Also written by Tom Bird
WILLY STARGELL: AN AUTOBIOGRAPHY (with Willy Stargell)

Phil Niekro
and
Tom Bird

FREUNDLICH BOOKS
NEW YORK

Library of Congress Cataloging-in-Publication Data

Niekro, Phil, 1939–
Knuckle balls.
1. Niekro, Phil, 1939– . 2. Baseball players—
United States—Biography. I. Bird, Tom, 1956–
II. Title.
GV865.N5A3 1986   796.357′092′4 [B]   86-9902
ISBN 0-88191-042-2

Published by Freundlich Books
212 Fifth Avenue
New York, NY 10010

Distributed to the trade by Kampmann & Company, Inc.
9 East 40th Street
New York, N.Y. 10016

Manufactured in the United States of America

10 9 8 7 6 5 4 3 2 1

This book is dedicated to my parents, Mr. and Mrs. Phil Niekro of Lansing, Ohio. No parents have ever meant more to their son than my parents mean to me. Because of their constant influence and presence I consider myself the luckiest man in the world.

Phil Niekro

I dedicate my work to the memory of my father, James Bird, who taught me about the game of life through his teachings to me of baseball.

Tom Bird

ACKNOWLEDGMENTS

The writing of a book such as this cannot be done by two people alone. The love, help and assistance of several hundred others, or maybe, in this case, thousands of others, is needed.

First, we'd like to thank those individuals who have played a significant part in our pasts and without whose inspiration and faith this book would have never become reality. Thus to those individuals, the entire town of Lansing, Ohio, and all the inhabitants of the beautiful Ohio Valley who've had so much of an impact on both Phil's life and career; all Phil's fellow students at Bridgeport High School and St. Joseph's Catholic Grade School, his coaches and fellow athletes, the Atlanta Braves, especially Ted Turner, without whose assistance the true story behind Phil's release would have been forever a mystery; the New York Yankees, especially Joe Safety, the game's finest PR man who both of us consider a very close and dear friend; our friends at the Loews Glenpoint Hotel in Teaneck, New Jersey, who made working on this book so entertaining; and Bruce Church, Phil's agent and one of his best friends, a true man of integrity and distinction, whom without the assistance of, this book would have never gotten off the ground; we say "thank you."

On the literary side, we'd like to thank Jay Acton, our literary representative, who saw the true validity in our idea and had the wisdom to see the project through; his assistant Inge Hanson; Larry Freundlich, our publisher, whose creative spirit has made this book the success that it is; and the managerial excellence of Deborah Freundlich, who makes ideas book realities.

We'd also like to give due credit to our family members who put up with us and helped us through the writing of this book: Phil's brother, Joe, and sister, Phyllis, who added not only their own version of comic relief but also helped us jar Phil's memory on more than one occasion; Phil's sons, Philip, John and Michael, who were always a constant source of inspiration; Phil's lovely wife Nancy, without whose help this book would still be in the writing stage; and to my wife Amy, who is and always will be a constant source of inspiration and enthusiasm for me .To all of you we say "thank you." Again, we couldn't have done it without you.

PHIL NIEKRO
TOM BIRD

PREFACE

Ted Turner and Phil Niekro have done a lot for one another and Atlanta baseball. But, when Turner betrayed Niekro by selling him to the New York Yankees, he not only banished his most valuable baseball commodity, but poisoned a friendship once treasured by the great pitcher and the great entrepreneur.

I visited Ted Turned shortly before our book was prepared for press.

"I fucked up," he said.

"It was a mistake. And it was my fault. It was a collective decision, but I was the one who made the *final* decision. I was the one who fucked up.

"We thought Phil was through. He was only an 11–10 pitcher that year."

What Turner did not take into consideration was that Niekro, even at 45, was still the club's second-leading winner in 1983, that he had won his last seven decisions, and had had an amazing 17–4 record the year before. If Turner had treated the Niekro situation with the same intelligence and avarice that he treats his other businesses, there no way he would have let the Braves' star pitcher go.

"I would have kept him if he was only five or six wins from 300," says Turner. "But he was somethin' like 25 or 30 away at the time, and there was no way that we thought he could win that many for us. He just had too many injuries that year that would have affected his performance. . . ."

The injuries that Turner refers to are leg injuries, which Niekro suffered in '82, the result of aggressive headfirst slides that sometimes pulled or strained his hamstrings. *His arm was as good as ever.*

When Ted Turner refers to the "we" who banished Niekro, he is ducking behind a conglomeration of his top generals, a group which has included Joe Torre, the manager, his pitching coach, Bob Gibson, and the rest of Torre's coaching staff.

"A rat got between us," says Niekro. "I think that Joe saw me as a threat to his job. So he and his coaches just wanted to get rid of me to save their own asses. It was no secret that Ted had talked to me about managing the Braves. And I think that they were scared that Ted was gonna fire Joe and hire me, and then that I'd fire them."

The Braves suffered severely from Phil's banishment. Having become one of the best clubs in the Western Division of the National League (in 1982 they were champs of the division, and in 1983 they were a close second), they floundered immediately after Niekro's banishment, plunging ingloriously into the second division.

In Turner's own words, "He was the Braves. If I would have known what I know now, I would never have let him go. I never thought that he'd go on to win that many games with the Yankees."

Why then didn't Turner try to re-sign him after last year with the Yankees? The journalists were expecting that he would, and the Braves' fans were praying for it.

Turner *did*, in fact, make Niekro an offer. Ted Turner offered Phil Niekro a job as a minor league manager. Turner told me that, after receiving the offer, "Phil turned his back and mooned us. . . ."

"Our decision not to re-sign Phil was basically a decision made by my baseball people, Bobby Cox and Chuck Tanner. *I was too busy with this MGM thing to get involved.* I guess they just didn't understand that Phil could be of any use to us."

No matter what Torre, Gibson, and the rest did to get rid of Niekro, the responsibility for Niekro's release falls on Ted Turner, a man who is not unfamiliar with acting like a boss.

Turner had every opportunity to right these wrongs by re-signing Phil at the conclusion of the 1985 season. He had given Niekro every indication that he would. But now Turner says:

"I'll be surprised if Niekro makes the Yankee team this spring. In fact, I'll be surprised if he even pitches again. That is, unless another team picks him up after the Yankees cut him. *When is he going to learn that you can't pitch forever?*"

If, as he claims, Turner banished Niekro for business reasons— meaning Niekro's usefulness as a pitcher had been used up by age—that same business mentality should have made Ted Turner know enough to bring Niekro back to Atlanta to win historic game No. 300 in front of the Atlanta loyalists, who churn the turnstiles and make the advertising rates of both CNN and WTBS so valuable.

Turner had neither the courage of his business convictions, the moxie of a baseball man, nor the character of a friend. Instead, both the glory and the bucks went to mild-mannered George Steinbrenner, who showcased Phil, not only because Niekro was filling Yankee Stadium, but also because Niekro is a winning pitcher.

PROLOGUE FROM CLEVELAND

When Steinbrenner threw me out of the Yankee camp, I was confused and mad as hell. Maybe I'd been offered a contract for the new season because the Yankees really wanted to keep my brother Joe in camp. Maybe they wanted to get all the spring-training head-lines that having 47-year-old Phil Niekro in camp would bring them.

I pitched my heart out for the Yankees. I won 32 games for them over two seasons. I brought out the crowds in pursuit of my historic 300th win.

It seems that wasn't enough for the Yankees.

You can't imagine the sense of loneliness of being out of it when still a winning major league pitcher, I wasn't chosen from the waiver list. Everybody asked, "What's his age?", not, "Can he still pitch?"

Only Cleveland asked, "Can he still pitch?" And they came up with the right answer: you bet the hell he can. Wholehearted thanks go out to Cleveland. But Cleveland did us BOTH a favor. One is a baseball favor: they got a pitcher who is going to win important games for them. The other one is a favor you might even call moral: they judged me as a man, not by my age.

In this book you're going to read a lot about how the Yankees and the Braves never understood the drive behind the old Polack, and just who in those organizations seem hell-bent on making baseball blunders or just plain human blunders.

But this season is not one in which I'm going to look back on the bad things. It's a season I'm going to pitch my heart out for the Indians, not only because I always pitch that way, but because Cleveland treated me like a man.

Phil Niekro

Sunday, October 6, 1985 — TORONTO

No. 300. To Pitch or Not to Pitch

As far as I was concerned, I had the perfect reason not to pitch today if I wanted. We weren't playin' in New York, we were outta the pennant race. Toronto had already won, and one win wouldn't matter either way for us. I had the perfect reason not to pitch, which kinda solved a dilemma for me anyways. Cause all season long I struggled with the situation of where I'd like to win No. 300. I felt I owed it to George and the Yankees for giving me the chance. But in my heart, I wanted to win it for Atlanta.

I had already made up my mind during spring training that if we fell out of the pennant race, and I still had a chance to win No. 300, that I'd ask George to trade me back to Atlanta so I could win it there. And the way it looked sometimes, and from all the headlines I read about the Braves, it looked as if I might be going back there not only to play but also to manage. That would've solved the entire situation. But it never came about. And here I found myself stuck with this mess, with my heart in Atlanta, my butt in these pinstripes and a chance for No. 300 on the line.

But after yesterday's loss, Joe and I went out with a few old buddies to have some drinks and I got to thinkin'. As much as it looked as if I'd be a Brave next year and as much as I wanted to win No. 300 in Atlanta, who was to guarantee that I'd be with Atlanta next season. Stranger things have happened, like when the Braves released me. And even though Ted Turner repeatedly told me over the last two years how he thought the biggest mistake he'd ever made was letting me go, there was still no guarantee that I'd be back with 'em.

Then I got to thinkin'. Well, if they don't sign me after the season, and the Yankees haven't talked to me about a contract yet, maybe I won't be signed. Again, stranger things have happened. There aren't too many guys who've won as many games over a two-year span as I have. Maybe this could be my last chance at No. 300.

I also got to thinkin' about my dad. At his age and in his condition, how could I even be sure that he'd be around next spring to see me pitch? I knew he wanted to see me win No. 300, and he deserved to 'cause he was as much a part of my success as anyone. With all that on my mind, I still went to bed last night thinkin' that I had a perfect excuse not to pitch today if I didn't want to. And in my heart I really didn't want to go out there today because I wanted to win No. 300 in Atlanta.

But when I woke up this morning after tossin' and turnin' over all the alternatives, I felt that I had better take the chance while it was still there. For, like I said, with this crazy game of ours, even though I'd won over 30 games the last two years, who knows if I'd ever get another chance.

When I got to the ball park today, a good portion of the guys were either packin' to leave or had planned to leave early. Nobody seemed to really give a shit but me. But in my mind, I realized that this may be my last game, but I was ready.

As I walked out to the bullpen to warm up, I was greeted by a nice round of applause by the crowd, most of whom still looked a little hungover from the night before. But I got a real nice feeling from 'em, a real warm feelin'. They were there to see me pitch—and to win.

In the bullpen, I told Butch Wynegar that I wanted to start the first few guys out on hard stuff. As far as I was concerned, with the way these guys were probably out celebratin' last night, a knuckler might look straight to them. Plus, I wanted to show, not only myself, but also everybody else, and all those guys that said that the only thing that kept me in the game all these years was my knuckler, that I was more than a knuckleball pitcher. I wanted to show them them that I deserved to be where I was, that I deserved to win 300 games.

I even remember a conversation that I had with Billy Martin a few months ago, when I told him that if I ever got the chance to go after No. 300 that I'd like to win it without throwin' a knuckler. He just laughed. Not even he believed me.

I zipped right through the first four innings. No knucklers. By that time, we had a 3–0 lead. In the dugout, Joe asked me, "When ya gonna throw one?" Not even my own brother believed that I could do it. I just looked at him and laughed.

In the sixth, we were ahead 5–0 and Willie Randolph came over to the mound with this real shit eatin' grin on his face.

"What the hell's goin' on here," he asked?

"Not gonna throw one," I said.

"Go for it," he exuberantly yelled.

By the ninth, with us ahead 8–0, the word was pretty much out. Niekro hadn't thrown a knuckleball yet. Before I headed out to the mound to face the Jays for the last time, I told Joe that if I lost the shutout that I was gonna take myself outta the game so he could finish for me. So he could share in the experience too. He told me to shove that thinkin' up my ass.

I threw my first knuckler of the afternoon when Joe came out to warm me up. The sucker handcuffed him cause he wasn't expectin' it and almost hit him in the nuts.

With only three outs to go, I could feel the tenseness of the crowd, the bench, the bullpen. As I set up to take the sign from Butch for the first batter, all of a sudden, the home plate ump throws up his arms and calls time out.

Just then I looked over toward our dugout, where Billy is just laughin' his ass off, as five guys go trottin' down to our bullpen, like I needed the help. I wondered to myself whose side that little son of a gun was on anyway.

But I didn't let his antics bother me. I wanted this one. I wanted this one for me. I set down the first two guys, no problem, also no knuckleballs.

Then Bobby Cox sent up Tony Fernandez to pinch-hit. He doubled to left. Then Jeff Burroughs, who was with me from the Braves, stepped up to the plate. I took the sign from Butch, and then again the ump threw his hands up.

This time Joe came trottin' out to the mound and said that Billy wanted to know if I wanted to pitch to Burroughs or not? I just looked back at him and said, "I want this guy."

Butch gave me the first sign again. Fastball. Burroughs was waitin' on it but got ahead of it and pulled it way off into the left-field stands. I think I surprised him with my dwindling velocity. Butch set down another sign, another fastball. But this time I buzzed Burroughs up high and tight.

Butch set down another sign, a fastball. I shook it off. I wanted the knuckler. Not because I didn't think I could win without it, but because I just couldn't see pitching the most important game of my career, which may also be the last game of my career, without throwing one.

Butch laughed, and Burroughs swung wildly and missed. Butch set down another sign, another knuckler. Burroughs swung wildly again and then turned slowly from the plate and walked away. The game was over. *I did it, and I did it my way.*

Joe was the first one to run out to the mound to greet me, and right then and there he told me the best news that I had ever heard.

"Dad's outta intensive care," he said. "They just took him out a few hours ago. It looks like he's gonna be fine."

Back inside the clubhouse, two bottles of champagne waited for me, one from George, the other from Ted.

Wednesday, October 5, 1983

I got out of my blazer and walked over toward the entrance to Ted's office at WTBS, where a local Atlanta newspaper reporter, Chris Morrison, was waiting.

"Whattya think the meeting's 'bout, Knucksie?" he asked.

Hell, I didn't know. All I knew was that Dee, Ted's secretary, had called me a few days ago and asked me if I could meet with Ted this morning, and that's what I told Morrison.

But deep inside I was kinda wonderin' the same thing, too. This all seemed like kind of a mystery to me. I mean, I'd been with the Braves for nearly twenty years and I'd been their top pitcher for most of that time, too. And even when they didn't win, I still did.

Yet, I still felt really strange. I hadn't had the best season last year, but then it wasn't bad either. I had had my usual slow, shitty start, but after I got the bugs out of my old body, I was once again pitching like the Phil Niekro of old. And in the second half of the season, I was the team's best pitcher. But, still, there hadn't been any contract talks. And at the end of the season, there wasn't that old reliable feeling inside me saying, "See ya next year." That's why I felt so confused and why I really didn't know what to expect that morning. All I knew was that Ted wasn't gonna be asking me to bat leadoff next year.

I walked inside Ted's office to find him and an expressionless John Mullen waiting for me, and right then and there I knew something was up.

Ted just wasn't himself. I mean, the man standing before me was not the Ted Turner that I had grown to know and love, the guy who I had drunk beer with, fished with. This was not the Ted Turner I had so often sat up all night swapping stories with, the man that I had watched learn to chew tobacco, the Ted Turner that I felt as close to as anyone I had ever known. This was not Ted. To begin with, he was nervous.

I mean, why the hell should a guy like Ted, a guy who is one of the country's most affluent and flamboyant individuals, a guy who even the Russians won't fool with, be made to feel so nervous in the presence of a forty-four-year-old—soon to be forty-five-year-old—jockstrap? I kinda felt as if he was gonna tell me that I had incurable knuckle cancer or somethin'.

"*Ahhhhhhhhh, welllll, ummmmmmmmm, ahhh, wellll, ahh,* Phil," he started. Since when had I been so intimidating? Hell, I know little leaguers who wouldn't back away from my fastball.

"*Ahhhh, welll, ahhhhh,* Phil. . . ." Then I started to worry about Ted's health. Maybe he was the one with the terminal cancer. And a man his age! Right in the prime of his life! What a pity! I just kinda wanted to go over and throw my arms around him.

"Well, *ahh,* me and the rest of the, well, the *ummmmmm,* club's decision makers"—I hoped he hadn't spoken to Brezhnev this way on his last trip to Moscow—"had a meeting and well, *ummmm,* we kinda feel that, well, I guess we, *ahhhh,* unanimously decided that, well, you should retire."

What me? I'm only forty-five! So that's what this shit is about, huh! I just kept thinking to myself, "Who are these fucking decision makers, Ted? You own the goddamn club! Who can tell *you* what to do?"

Then I looked over at Mullen, sitting there so proud and sturdy, obviously representing the silent majority. Then a few things began to fall into place.

Someone had finally gotten to Ted, huh? They'd somehow gotten to him and convinced him that for the good of the Braves, it would be better if I was gone. But the truth of the matter is that I think the fact that I had been strongly considered for the manager's job at one time had something to do with their decision to try and force me to retire. I just think that all of them would have felt a hell of a lot securer if I was gone.

And here's Ted, the most honest, trustworthy individual I had ever met, standing up in front of me trying to make this all sound like a group decision. I just cannot believe that Ted had anything to do with this. This was not the Ted Turner that I had known so well for so long.

Then Mullen started babbling in. "It's not that we don't think you can pitch anymore, that's not it at all. And it's not your age either. In fact, we still think you can win."

"Just give me my release papers then," I said, somewhat surprising everyone present, including myself, which kinda brought Ted back around.

"Well, wait a minute, Phil," Ted chimed in. "If you think you can still pitch, I'll take you to spring training with the club. As far as I'm concerned, you'll always have a place with the Braves as long as I'm here."

"Ted," I said, as I stood to leave, "I ain't goin' to spring training holding nobody's hand and I don't expect to get a chance to pitch just 'cause I'm your friend. Just give me my release papers and I'll find a job somewhere else."

I grew up in Lansing, Ohio, though I was actually born in Blaine, Ohio, which is a tiny town right down the road. Compared to Blaine, Lansing is a metropolis. At the peak of the vacation season, it houses approximately 1000 people. Both are coal-mining towns.

My dad, like his dad and almost every other man in the area, was a coal miner. In fact, the two towns were initially constructed simply because of the coal mines. But now with the mines shut down, there's basically no financial reason for either of the towns to exist, except for maybe the Melody Manor, the local drinking establishment, or Fritz's Barbershop and the Sportsman's Club, the area's two other local drinking establishments.

While the Manor specializes in fine food and spirits, Fritz's specializes in haircuts and homemade wine. Nobody really knows which Fritz's customers prefer the most. But one thing is for sure, if Fritz screws up your haircut, you don't realize it until the next morning, after the effects of the wine have worn off. And by that time, you don't really care.

Baseball in the Niekro blood goes way back. My dad was born in a row house that sat directly over an area that is presently occupied by home plate of the local baseball field. He just seemed to have an innate love for the game. By the time he was 16 years old, he was the hardest throwing, farthest hitting baseball player in the area. Folks used to come from miles around to see him play and he was always the highlight of the show.

Though he could hit a ball out of sight, my dad's strongest suit was still his pitching. Old-timers in the area still say that my dad was the finest pitcher they'd ever seen, even after seeing the likes of my brother Joe and me, and after watching a slew of big-league games in Pittsburgh, which is only about 70 miles to the north.

But my dad's hope for fame, fortune, and a big league career died at the young age of eighteen, when he blew out his arm on a chilly Sunday afternoon. Loaded with talent, but inadequately trained, my father had attempted to pitch that afternoon without warming up. Though his dream may have died that afternoon, his love for the game never did.

Around this same time, my dad met and married my mother. Both were orphans, which wasn't unusual for those times in tiny coal-mining towns like Lansing and Blaine, where the living was hard.

My dad's folks had died when he was relatively young, around 10 or so. And as was the routine, he was simply absorbed by the community and taken in by another family. Unfortunately, the wife of the man that took him in hated children, probably the reason she never had any of her own. As a result, she treated my father more like a slave than a son. He was rarely if ever fed, and was continually forced to do work which even slaves would've refused to do. But after a few months in that household, the town folk eventually heard of the agony that my father was being forced to live through and moved him in with another family.

My mom's parents died when she was about 16 years old, leaving behind not only my mom, but seven other children. My mom and dad met and married soon afterward. He was 18. She was 16.

Since he decided to take in some of my mom's brothers and sisters and raise them as his own, my father needed a much larger home than the one he was presently living in. So he moved his young wife and his inherited family into a much larger home, about a quarter of a mile up the road from where he was born.

Not long afterward, my sister, Phyllis, was born in that home. A few years later, I was born there also.

Then my parents purchased a house in Lansing, which was only a few miles down Interstate 40, which at that time was one of this country's main thoroughfares. The house was located directly off the interstate and bordered on a set of railroad tracks to the rear. To say the least, I grew up in a rockin' environment. If a truck wasn't shakin' the house from the front, then a train was from the back. Then sometimes, both would hit at the same time, causing the house to rock 'n roll like a carnival ride. With all the constant motion running through our home, I carried myself like a person walking through an epileptic fit.

But we had all the modern conveniences that a family could want at the time. We had a stove and icebox—and an outhouse in our backyard. The outhouse especially had an effect on my later years in athletics. For it instilled in me the finer points of grace and balance, skills that I inherited via nightly visits to it during the winter months, when I was often forced to skate barefooted across our frozen backyard to relieve myself.

Since we were basically lower blue collar, my parents were unable to provide us with much, as far as material goods are concerned, but they made up for that with their constant love, guidance, and affection. As far as my mom was concerned, that meant teaching us the values of honesty, modesty, and a strong inner faith and belief in the Almighty. On my father's side, that meant teaching us to throw the knuckler, which he'd taken up after blowing out his arm. It was the only family heirloom that he had to pass on.

My dad was so wowed over the prospect of being able to pass on the knuckler to us that he actually began teaching Phyllis to throw it even before she could walk. And as soon as I was born, he had me out in the backyard tossing it back and forth with him every night.

As I got older, I used to wait anxiously for him to get home from work each afternoon, so we could go out back and play. As soon as I saw him, I'd run down the driveway to meet him. He'd always be covered from head to toe with coal dust. He'd drop his lunch bucket on the back porch, pick me up and carry me into the backyard, where we'd play ball until sundown.

This was routine around the Niekro household. We were bound together as much by the knuckler as we were by our love for each other. It was just something that we all shared.

Eventually, Joe was born. But by this time, Phyllis had taken over the role as my catcher, a role that she fulfilled a whole hell of a lot better than some of the big leaguers I've had to work with over the years. I guess it must have just been in her genes. In fact, I think that if she had wanted to, and if a professional league for women existed, she could have easily won three hundred games. She was that good.

But as far as Joe is concerned, he really didn't take up the knuckler until he had already made it in the majors. As a kid his hands were just too small to be able to grip it properly. So he grew up throwing the hard stuff.

Eventually, Joe's hard stuff got him to the big leagues—with the Cubs, in 1967. But after a few decent years with Chicago, Joe just kinda fumbled around the majors and high minors until it looked as if he was gonna fall out of baseball completely. Then, and only then, did he adopt the knuckler. Though he struggled with it at first, he soon gained the confidence that he needed to throw it consistently and started winning 17, 18, 19, 20 games a year after that.

. . .

When I was growing up there, Lansing always seemed to breed a unique competitive spirit among its inhabitants, most of whom were first- or second-generation immigrants.

Besides Joe and myself, several other professional athletes also emerged from the area during the time we were growing up. Bill Jobko was one. Bill, who grew up about four blocks away from me, played football for Woody Hayes at Ohio State and was twice named MVP of the Rose Bowl. Bill eventually went on to conclude his career by playing in the NFL, where he is presently employed by the Atlanta Falcons.

But probably the most famous athlete to come out of Lansing was my close friend and schoolmate John Havlicek, or Yunch, as I used to call him, who, as a member of the Boston Celtics, later gained recognition as one of the greatest players ever to play in the NBA.

John was by far the greatest athlete ever to come out of the Lansing area. There was literally nothing that he couldn't do. On the gridiron, he was our high-school quarterback and was sought after by every major college in the country. On the diamond, he played shortstop and was highly regarded by almost every big-league scout that ever saw him play.

But John was even more dazzling on the basketball court, where he eventually led Ohio State to a national championship and the Celtics to many world championships. John used to get up at 6:00 A.M. every morning just so he could jog down to our school and squeeze in a few hours of practice before school began.

John's ability as an athlete and as a leader surfaced at a very early age. In fact, I remember that John's parents, who ran the local grocery store, never bought John a bicycle. But that didn't prove to be any problem for John, who just ran alongside, often for miles, as we all peddled to our destinations. On his more enthusiastic days, he even ran far out ahead of us.

John got the majority of the attention from the college and pro scouts that visited the area. To them, he was a super athlete. Me, I was just a knuckleball pitcher/first baseman.

While I was in high school, I got a lot of look-sees from scouts, but no takers. So I went to work for the Continental Can Company right out of high school and played legion league and semi-pro baseball whenever I could.

Finally, after about a year at the can company, a scout for the Pittsburgh Pirates invited me to a tryout camp at Forbes Field. I'll never forget climbing aboard that bus and heading for Pittsburgh. All my family and half the town were there to see me off. Mom had packed me lunch. It was the first bus ride of my life. I was excited as hell. I was probably the first person, with the exception of John, to dare venture out of the safe confines of the area in the last 50 years.

Playing for the Pirates would have been perfect. I'd be only seventy miles away from home. All my friends and family could take the bus up to see me play. And most were Pirates fans anyway. It was perfect. That was, until they sent me home empty handed.

When I got to the tryout camp, there were hundreds of players there, which only gave each of us a few minutes to showcase our skills. Which, when you're a knuckleball pitcher, means about three pitches. The son of a guns just don't get to the plate that fast.

The news fell hard on my family and friends. They'd all been pullin' for me for years. Mom, especially, just couldn't understand it. In fact, she harbors a grudge against the Pirates to this day.

So I continued to play semi-pro ball and work at the can company for another month or so, until I finally got my break. My team was playing another semi-pro team that had a few former pros. There were a couple of big-league scouts in the stands that night, and we were giving 'em quite a show. Finally, entering into the late innings with the score tied, the other team loaded up the bases with none out. Our coach took me off first base and brought me in to face the heart of their lineup, all three of whom had at one time been professional ballplayers. I struck out all three of 'em on nine pitches. Bill Maughn, of the Braves, came up to me after the game and invited me to a tryout camp Milwaukee was gonna be holding nearby.

After the tryout camp, Maughn offered me a contract for five hundred big ones, which I gladly signed. Hell, the selling price for the entire town of Lansing at the time was only $1500. I thought that I was rolling in dough.

Since I was signed at the end of the summer, the Braves thought it would be best if I didn't report to one of their teams until the following spring. So I continued to work at the can company and play semi-pro ball in the area, which really ticked off some of the other managers and players, since I'd already signed a professional contract and all. But heck, there just isn't that much to do in Lansing. And since the radio at the local gas station, where we used to stand around and listen to ball games and watch cars go by every evening, had gone on the fritz, I had nothing else to do.

The following spring, after a glorious forty-hour bus ride, I anxiously arrived at the Braves training camp in beautiful Waycross, Georgia.

I was amazed by the number of players that the Braves had in camp. There were hundreds of players there, each assigned to separate barracks-like buildings, appropriately referred to as tee-pees. There were about forty guys assigned to a teepee, many of whom were hardened veterans. To them I was a greenhorn—and instantly became their primary source of entertainment for the next few months.

I just wanted to be a big leaguer in the worst way, and I guess that I must have stood out. When we were told to take a few laps on the running track, most of the guys just jogged; I sprinted. When we were told to throw for a certain amount of time, I always threw for twice as long.

As a result, by the end of the day, I usually just fell asleep in my bunk and slept right through dinner and right into the next morning. And I mean, I could sleep. Once in high school I fell asleep during football practice. Back then, my ability to sleep soundly brought a round of laughter. But in this circumstance, it brought the worst outta these guys.

Once, my teepeemates put shoe polish all over my hands and then tickled my face with a feather. I woke up the next morning looking like Bill Cosby. Then another time they painted all my toenails and fingernails with hot pink nail polish, and I took the field the next morning looking like a cheap whore.

But the worst thing that they did to me was when they put one of my hands in a bowl of warm water, causing me to awake suddenly in the middle of the night and run for the men's room with my one hand securely holding my crotch.

But they began to accept me by the end of camp, or at least that's what I thought. In fact, some of the guys even asked me and this other guy, who they also considered a greenhorn, purely by coincidence I thought, to go snipe hunting, which they described as the capturing of elusive little black birds with paper bags. Being the avid sportsman that I was, I was anxious to go.

When the much-awaited evening finally arrived, they drove me and the other guy out into an area located in the middle of a dark, gloomy swamp, a couple of miles from camp, and proceeded to tell us about the finer points of capturing snipe. Then they led us to what appeared to be a predetermined area in the swamp, handed us our paper bags and promised to spread out in several directions to shoo the snipe toward us. Since we were newcomers, they said that it was the least they could do to let us catch the first snipe of the evening. We were both extremely grateful for their generosity. We never saw them again, or at least not that evening. In fact, the next time we saw them was when we came chugging back into camp the next morning, a few hours before wake-up time, after our hike back from the swamp. Again, they were laughing their asses off.

At the end of camp, we were divided into different teams composing different levels of advancement. I was assigned to the Wellsville, New York team, the lowest rung in the Braves' organizational ladder. I was the last player placed on their roster. I was the lowest of the low.

A few weeks later, we boarded an old school bus that the owner of the Wellsville team had sent to fetch us and began our journey up north. The bus looked like one of those ones that poor churches always use. It was about thirty-seven different colors and had to be at least fifty years old. At times, it grunted and groaned each time the driver shifted up or down, depending on the direction of his shift. And when we came to any hill of substantial size, we all had to get out and walk up the hill, 'cause the bus could never make it with us aboard. But heck, I was just glad to be there. I would've climbed a thousand hills and put hot pink nail polish all over my body if that's what it would have taken to become a big leaguer.

I was doin' O.K. in Wellsville. I mean, I hadn't been invited on any more snipe hunting expeditions and I hadn't woken up with shoe polish all over my face. Then one day as I was walking to the park, I noticed a big car, loaded down with suitcases and personal belongings, parked in front of the local hotel.

In those days, teams didn't just release a player, they sent him down from level to level until he finally played himself out of baseball. And each time a player was sent down to a lower level, another player had to be sent down to the level below him. Until things finally reached the end of the line, where I was, and someone had to be released. That person in this case, happened to be me.

My manager called me into his office the next day and told me the news. I just broke down and started to cry, started to plead, to beg him to take me back or at least get me sent to another team. I just didn't want to have to go home this way. I didn't want to have to leave the luxury of professional baseball. Hell, they don't have buses as nice in Lansing like that one we rode in from Waycross to here.

After a few minutes of listening to me plead, he got on the phone, and the next thing I knew I was on a train headed for McCook, Nebraska, where the Braves had just opened up a Rookie League team, the new low rung on the ladder. I arrived in McCook a few days later, stepped out of the train at 6:00 A.M., immediately boarded the team's bus, and was off on my first road trip.

Thursday, October 6, 1983

The elevator ride down to the clubhouse was probably the longest I ever took. When the doors finally opened, a swarm of cameramen and reporters were waiting for me, but I just ducked my head and walked toward the clubhouse, grabbed a few cardboard boxes and headed for my locker, still somewhat too confused and hurt to talk.

As clear and concise as my meeting had been yesterday, I still felt overwhelmingly confused. I just couldn't understand it. Hell, I would have played for Ted for free. In fact, my wife Nancy and I even talked about me doing so one night. After all that Ted had done for us and our family, we thought it would be a perfect way to show our appreciation.

But my old buddy Skip Caray, who we bounced the idea off of, thought I was a real dumb ass to even consider such a venture. "Why give up one year of your life for nothin'?" he asked. And he was right. At my age, you don't have that many years left to be giving them away so freely.

As I tossed my stuff into the boxes, for the first time in my life I felt really alone. But for some reason, I felt that I would be returning to this clubhouse somehow, some way.

In fact, I was just tempted to scratch a little mark inside my locker that said: LEFT—OCTOBER 6, 1983; RETURNED—198?, but there were just too many reporters around. So, instead, I just went home and had a few.

The McCook club was a team especially created for the Braves' higher-priced signees who needed a little extra seasoning before being moved up. Most of the guys on the club carried more money in their pockets than I had originally been paid to sign. In McCook, though I didn't fit in financially, I did pitch pretty well and made my first real close friend in the game.

His name was Carl Derr. Carl and I and this other guy shared an apartment in the basement of the Mohr's home in McCook, and as part of our after-game, nightly entertainment, we used to play penny-ante poker. It was about all that we could afford.

Well, this other guy just kept winning and winning for what seemed like weeks, and Carl and I were getting real suspicious. Finally, Carl and I decided to call his bluff. So we called for a count of the cards in the middle of one of the games. A few were missing. We found them under his leg. Immediately, we just began tossing his belongings out of the apartment. Everybody on the team had heard about what happened the next day, even our manager, who asked us to verify the story. A few days later, the guy was released. They take penny-ante poker real seriously in the bushes.

The next year I was promoted to Jacksonville, where I was used primarily as a reliever again. Then, at the end of the season, I was elevated to Louisville, which was the Braves' highest-ranking farm team. But the next year, I was sent down to Austin, where I pitched well again. It just seemed like they really didn't know what to do with me, like they just kept switching me around while they tried to decide.

Finally, in '62, I was put on the Louisville roster to stay. While there, I noticed that at almost every game a large group of Army Reserve Troops, who were stationed at nearby Fort Knox, would be in attendance. Never did I imagine that I'd be among them, but the next year I was.

As soon as they heard at Fort Knox that I was a professional ballplayer, they asked me to join their team, a team that hadn't beaten its rival in somethin' like twenty years. I guess that they kinda saw me as the guy that was gonna break their streak for them. So I was given special privileges. In fact, I wasn't expected to do anything at all. Everybody knew that, except my sergeant, who was so drunk most of the time that he probably didn't even know his own name.

Well, one time he put my name on the duty roster for KP the next morning. So I got up at three-thirty in the morning, as was expected of me, and was in the kitchen peeling potatoes and cracking egg at 4:00 A.M., when the lieutenant who was in charge of the baseball team walked in. He was furious and immediately sent me back to my barracks.

An hour later, my sergeant was called in by the company commander. Shortly after, red-eyed and lookin' stewed as ever, he returned and woke me from a deep sleep.

"Neeho," he said in his usual slurred fashion, "I've been in this fuckin' army for twenty fuckin' years and I ain't never had my ass chewed out like I just had it chewed out this morning. And I'll tell you one thing right now, goddamnit, I don't give a shit if you ever do another goddamn thing around here ever again. I don't even give a shit if you sleep all goddamn day. I don't care if you need a pass or need to go somewhere. Just see me an' you've got it. 'Cause I ain't never gonna be chewed out like that again."

Needless to say, my stay in the service was something of a piece of cake. I simply pitched us into the camp finals that year and then found myself with the Milwaukee Braves in spring training the next year.

I came north with the Braves that year and stayed with them until the first cutdown, when I was sent down to Denver, which had replaced Louisville as their number one farm club. But by that time, I'd seen enough of Milwaukee to fall in love with the city. It was my kind of place. It was a blue-collar town with a lot of Pollacks, and there was a family-owned tavern on almost every street corner. You could get a shot of whiskey for a quarter and a beer for fifteen cents. It was my kind of town. I couldn't wait to get back up there.

I had another good year in Denver and was recalled again by the Braves at the end of the season, this time to stay. Then after a good year with the Braves in '65, I again made the club in '66, but this time as a member of the Atlanta Braves. But about halfway through that season, I was sent down to Richmond, which may have seemed like a demotion at first, but actually worked out to be one of the best moves of my life.

For while playing for Richmond, I met my wife, Nancy. She was a stewardess on one of our flights. And though I was engaged to a girl back home, the first time I laid eyes on Nancy, I told my buddy Gene Oliver, "I'm gonna marry that girl." Though he'd heard me say that hundreds of times before, this time he had reason to believe me, 'cause this was the first time he ever heard me say it sober.

Eventually, I got Nancy to play me in a game of cards. Not only did she win somethin' like two million dollars from me, but she also won my heart. I then thought that the only way that I would be able to repay her was to marry her, which I did before the end of the season.

We were married in Richmond, where Phyllis and her family lived, while the team was playing in Toronto. Our honeymoon consisted of a one-night stay in a motel, an elegant dinner consisting of greasy hamburgers, and concluded the next day with us driving another player's car back to Atlanta, where I'd been recalled that weekend. I never again went back to the minor leagues and everything just seemed to improve for me, most of which I attribute to Nancy, who always had faith in me and taught me to reach higher and to expect more of myself.

The next year I posted an 11–9 record with Atlanta and led the league with a 1.87 ERA. By this time, the Braves were finally starting to see some validity in using me as a starter. In fact, Paul Richards, the Brave's general manager, went out and got Bob Uecker from the Cardinals, just to catch me. Ueck became the first in a long line of catchers tailored especially for my needs, good defensive catchers with a great sense of humor.

When Ueck joined us, it was no real secret what the team's intention was for him, and nobody was happier for him than Joe Torre, our everyday catcher, who gave Ueck the ol' white carpet treatment by laying out a path of towels right to his locker, above which stood two signs, one from Joe and the other supposedly from me.

Torre's read: THANK YOU VERY MUCH. GOD BLESS YOU.

Mine said: LOTS OF LUCK, YOUR BUDDY, PHIL NIEKRO.

Ueck caught each one of my starts for the remainder of the season. And more than anyone else on the professional level, he was responsible for my success. He engrained in my mind that I shouldn't be afraid to throw the knuckler. What happened to it after it left my hand was not my responsibility, but instead his. As a result, he gave me that extra bit of confidence that I needed to get my career over the top. He helped me to my first real successful season in the big leagues and made it sound as if I alone was responsible for my league-leading ERA. Meanwhile, he took total responsibility for his league-leading twenty-seven passed balls.

But like everyone else, I remember the funny stories associated with Bob Uecker more than anything else; and one story especially sticks out in my mind. I had just beaten the Phillies this one night by a 2–1 score and I was gettin' a rubdown by our trainer, Harvey Stone, when a newspaper reporter walked in. Now, Harvey was a damn good trainer and he was always real proud of what good shape he kept all of us in. That night he told the reporter that he thought that I could start again the next day if I wanted to.

"No he couldn't," interrupted Paul Richards, who was standing nearby.

"Why not?" asked the surprised reporter.

" 'Cause Uecker needs at least four more days rest," he replied.

Ueck was released at the end of the season. But I'll always remember him as the guy who taught me what I needed to know about the knuckler: "Just throw the damn thing. Don't worry, I'll take the responsibility for chasing it down."

Then two years later, in '69, it all seemed to come together for both me and the Braves. First of all, Richards traded Torre for Orlando Cepeda, who had a really big year for us. Then he got Clete Boyer from the Yanks and brought up a catcher from the minors named Bob Didier, who had one hell of a year both at the plate and catching me.

I won twenty-three games that year and pitched twenty-one complete games, while Henry Aaron, Rico Carty, Felix Millan, Felipe Alou and the rest of the guys just kept putting runs on the board. We won the National League West that year but lost by a 3–0 margin to the Amazing Mets in the League Championship Series.

The next year we just went down the tubes. Everybody just seemed to have off years, which eventually led to the demise of the enitre Braves organization. I, especially, had a terrible year, which was mostly the result of having undergone an emergency appendectomy in the off-season. Then I tried to hurry back too quickly that spring and just wound up having a terrible year. My weight ballooned up to 208, I lost eighteen games, and led the league by giving up forty homers. The only thing that kept me from losing twenty and giving up fifty homers was Paul Richards, who sent me down to the instructional league for the last month of the season.

Our fall to fifth place that season was something that the club was unable to recover from for the next ten years. It seemed that we always had good individual stars but a lousy team. Soon we became the team that everybody wanted to play against, the team every batter wanted to hit against, and the team that every pitcher wanted to face. We became the shithole of the South. As a result, we began going through managers quicker than George Steinbrenner goes through secretaries.

Even in '74, when I won twenty games, the best we could do was finish in third place. The next year we finished in fifth. From that point forward, for the next five seasons, we finished last in the division.

By this time, Bill Bartholomay, the club's owner, wanted to

unload the club. One night he walked up to a young Ted Turner at one of the team's games and said, "I'm gonna sell the Braves."

"Who's gonna buy 'em," asked Turner.

"You are," replied Bartholomay, and a while later we had ourselves a new owner.

We really didn't know what to make of Ted. All we really knew was that he was a local TV-station owner. But he seemed real committed to making us into a winner. In fact, when he first took over, he promised the fans that he would have a World Champion in Atlanta in the next four or five years.

Then he immediately went out and started getting the players that he thought he could build a winner around. At about the same time, Ted started taking a real personal interest in all of us and our families. He started giving the guys off-season jobs and started training us for careers outside of baseball. He even offered to help us invest our money. In fact, in private he once told us to put any extra money we had in WTBS stock. Unfortunately, yours truly didn't listen.

I think the key, though, to Ted finally winning our confidence was when he took up chewing tobacco. By then he'd already made numerous appearances in the clubhouse wearing his levis and boat shoes, but it was tobacco that finally did it for Ted. From then on, we realized that we were more to him than just a tax write-off.

By 1982, Ted had revised his initial approach of trying to build the club through free agency and had instead gone to trying to build a winner from within, via the farm system. At that time, Bobby Cox, who's a great developer of young talent, was our manager.

Bobby was the guy who was primarily responsible for making Dale Murphy, Bob Horner, Glenn Hubbard, Rafael Ramirez, and the rest of the young Braves at the time into the players they have become. But I don't think the team was coming along fast enough for Ted, so he fired Bobby after the '81 season and hired Joe Torre as his new manager, a job that I had been considered for. By that time, Ted and I had become very close friends, and he made it known to me that I would someday be managing his team, a fact that Torre was also well aware of.

When Joe took over that spring, all the pieces just seemed to fall into place and we started off the season by winning our first thirteen games. We wound up winning the pennant that year but got beat 3–0 by the Cardinals in the championship series. Even though there were a lot of problems between the players, Joe, and his coaches, Joe still did a hell of a job that year and was deservedly named the National League's Manager of the Year. Murph was named the league's Most Valuable Player, and I went 17–4, one of the best records of my career.

The next year, there wasn't any real reason that we shouldn't have won it all again. We again got off to a good start but in the early going we just couldn't seem to get out of second place. I think that Joe then began to feel pressure of some kind. I was having my usual slow start, the same one that I'd had for the last twenty years, and frankly Joe felt that I was challenging for his job when I really wasn't. A coach or two also started reacting negatively toward me. In fact, Bob Gibson, our pitching coach, even told a couple of reporters about halfway through the season that he thought I was too old and should retire right then and there.

As the season wore on, the gap between Joe and me seemed to widen. He started pulling me out of games that he normally would have left me in. By the end of the season, I got the distinct feeling that I wouldn't be returning the following year.

Monday, January 6, 1984

Slumber parties are for teenagers, not for forty-four-year-old knuckleballers, and that's exactly how I felt about St. Louis' offer. They were willing to give me a good salary and a one-year contract, but they weren't willing to give me a single room on the road. And I mean, we're only talking an extra $500–600 a year for a little extra privacy.

Hey, I'm not thirteen years old anymore. If I want to pick my ass or fart, I don't want to be responsible for saying "ex*cuuuse* me." For at my age, that shit isn't funny anymore—it's rude. And I don't like to be considered fuckin' rude. So for the sake of my own sanity and also that of my prospective roomie, I felt as if I'd be better off alone. But the Cardinals didn't see it that way. "Club policy," they said.

"Good-bye!" I said.

Oakland was the next club to contact me. They had their pitching coach (and my old buddy) Ron Schueler, call. Nancy and his wife have been close friends for as long as I can remember.

Ron proceeded to tell me about all the good things playing in Oakland would have to offer me: a new club; a new league; a new coast; I wouldn't be able to see any of my old buddies from Atlanta or Ted, which would make leaving the Braves a whole lot easier.

Hey, playing for the A's sounded pretty good; and I was almost ready to pack my bags for Oakland, when Pittsburgh called. And what they had to offer sounded pretty temptin' too: I'd only be about seventy miles away from my folks and I could fly home to Atlanta on my off days for a barbecue or to guzzle a few beers with my buddies.

Then I got to thinkin'. "Wait a minute, Pittsburgh has got those goddamn ugly uniforms, with all those little gold circles around their caps and shit." But for all they had to offer, I figured I could bear the thought of stepping into one of their unis, that was until, of course, they brought up the partial trade contract.

"What's that?" I asked.

"Well, first you tell us the name of one team that we can't trade you to. Then we tell you the name of a club that we can trade you to. Then you give us the name of another team. And then we . . ."

"No thanks," I said. Though this type of arrangement may save me from playing in Candlestick, which would be just about every player's last choice, it still left the door open for me to be dealt to such paradises as Toronto and Montreal. No way.

Shortly after, my agent and close friend, Bruce Church, called.

"The big guy wants you," he said.

At first, I thought I was suffering through some sort of premonition and that my time to meet the Lord had come, you automatically start thinking like that when you get around my age, but then I realized that he meant George Steinbrenner of the Yankees.

The first thing I thought was, "No way." There's just no way

I'm gonna become just another puppet on Steinbrenner's purse strings. No way, not after all that shit I've heard about the Yankees, all the newspaper stories, and the firing of managers, the firing of bat boys, the firing of ball girls, ushers, janitors, and the firing of this and the firing of that. No way that old Bruce was gonna convince me into playing for the Yanks. Phil Niekro was not gonna become just another pawn in Steinbrenner's fanatical game of chess.

"I don't give a damn if they offer me five million dollars a year, Bruce, I'm not going!"

But then Nancy caught wind of the Yank's offer and she kinda liked the idea of me playing for the "Yankees." And she also kinda liked the idea of me being so close to home, as compared to Oakland. Then her and Bruce got to talkin' . . .

As I got out of the limousine at Yankee Stadium for the press conference to announce my signing, all I could say to myself was, "What the FUCK am I doing here?"

Monday, April 8, OPENING DAY—BOSTON

I'm the worst pitcher any manager could ever pick to start off a season with. In my over twenty very successful years in the bigs, I've accumulated an Opening Day record of 0–6. I guess Yog didn't know that. But screw it, I wasn't gonna tell him.

Instead, I just kept my mouth shut, slipped on my lucky KIELBASA POWER T-shirt under my jersey, and just went out there and got my ever-loving sausage knocked off. Make that 0–7 on Opening Days.

The Red Sox just jumped all over me. I just couldn't get my knuckler over. Hell, I'd only walked somethin' like six guys in all of spring training. Today, I walked five in only four innings. This forced me to use my blazing sixty-five mile per hour hummer in some tough situations, which the Sox neatly deposited either over or against the Green Monster. All in all, I gave up five runs in only four innings. Lucky T-shirt or not, I was horseshit!

On the other side of the coin, the Sox started this kid Dennis "Oil Can" Boyd. He's a real cocky son of a gun. In fact, after his antics today, the guys have begun referring to him as Shit Can.

For as skinny as he is, he sure has a lot of balls. He just kept humming it in there, right at our guys. He'd throw at our guys, knock 'em down, then stomp around the mound like Rocky or somethin'. But believe me, he did make two very critical mistakes. First, he chose our biggest, strongest guys—Baylor, Winfield, Mattingly—to throw at. And second, he embarrassed them terribly, and they're really pissed. His ass might just be ours by the time this season is over.

Our loss dropped us into last place in the division, with, of all teams, the Indians. Talk about being embarrassed. George won't be able to go to the country club for months.

Wednesday, April 10 — BOSTON

George bought Eddie Whitson on the free agent market over the winter. He was scheduled to be our starter today, and I think he's gonna fit right in. He's about as crazy as anyone here. Well, that is, with the exception of Joe Safety, our PR guy. Joe has been here two years. That's one year longer than any other PR man in the Steinbrenner era. Yes, I know it's hard to believe, but George has fired even more PR men over the years than managers. But Safety's a wild man. I think that's what he has over his predecessors.

Whit's just as loose as a goose around here. Yesterday, he put a rubber mouse in Gene Michael's shoe. Now Stick just hates slimy things. Hell, players playing practical jokes on him around here is a very big part of the Yankees tradition. It's been goin' on for generations. When Stick was still playin', someone even had the balls to put a hot dog in one of the fingers of his glove. Which just sent Stick through the roof, when he put the glove on his hand after takin' the field. Stuff like that happens to him all the time. Whit is just another player in a long line of pranksters who specialize in pickin' on Stick.

In case Whit's sore shoulder still bothered him, Guid went out to the bullpen today, too, and warmed up beside him, just in case he wouldn't be able to make it. But after awhile, Whit waved off Guid and headed into the game. And surprisingly, he even bettered my performance of yesterday. Hell, I looked like Cy Young compared to Whit today. Heck, he didn't even make it through the second inning before the Sox had lit him up for nine runs. At least that'll keep George off my back.

Whit later admitted that his back was still very sore when he went into the game, but he didn't want to miss his very first start as a Yankee. I hope he isn't gonna lose that crazy edge of his just because he's gettin' all that money. 'Cause that crazy, competitive edge is what got him here. I guess that's the major problem with players these days. We sign a big contract and think that we're supposed to change. But in reality, we've been given all that money just to do what we've been doin'.

I noticed in a New York newspaper today that a female cop in the city, a real looker, had been reinstated to her job after posing for some nude photos in a real sleazy porno magazine. Some of the other guys saw it, too. Hell, her picture was right on the front page. Me, I'm a married man so I wasn't interested, but some of the other guys said that they were gonna go over to her precinct after we got back in town and try to get arrested. Some guys'll do anything for a date.

Thursday, April 11—BOSTON

The look on George's face today in the *Post* said it all. He's pissed to say the least. Only two days and two losses into the season, he's already ready to hang all of us, especially Yog, who'd promised George that he'd get us off to a good start. Some guys'll say anything just to get George off their backs.

I'm sure that his disposition didn't improve much either, especially after we dropped our third game to the Red Sox today, 6–4. I wonder if it'd be possible for a big-league club to go through an entire season without winning even one game. I think that's what's on George's mind today.

Yog doesn't seem to be panicking though. He's got a multi-year contract. A reporter asked him today, "If today was crucial, what's tomorrow?"

Yog very calmly replied, "An off-day," proving that wit nullifies even fear.

Friday, April 12 — COLUMBUS

Some off-day! We had to spend the son of a gun in Columbus, Ohio, playin' an exhibition game against our AAA club. George just doesn't believe in off-days. Miraculously, over the years, he's been extremely consistent in his ability to schedule either workouts, charity luncheons, or exhibition games on all our off-days early in the season. That's just his way. He thinks that since the old-timers used to have to barnstorm their way north each spring, we should do so, too. I wish someone would advise him that they did so because they had to travel either by bus or train. And that we now travel by airplane, which makes such ventures a pain in the ass.

About the best part of the whole day for me was that I got to visit with my sister Phyllis and her family, who live here in Columbus. So I was kinda lookin' forward to comin' here. But nobody else was, and it showed. It was obvious that the guys were only goin' through the motions, nobody really seemed to care.

Like I said, it showed on the field. The Clippers just pummeled our tails, 14–5, which sent plenty of smoke flowing out of ol' Mount Steinbrenner. I'm sure that George grew especially dissatisfied with our effort when Juan Bonilla nonchalantly flipped a ball over pitcher Bob Shirley's head, which rolled to the dugout and allowed a run to score. While all the time this was taking place, Bonilla and Yog's son, Dale, stood at second base laughing.

Behavior like that could have really gotten us some headlines. I can just see it now: BERRA—THE FIRST YANKEE MANAGER IN HISTORY EVER FIRED FOR LOSING AN EXHIBITION GAME.

Saturday, April 13 — CLEVELAND

Thank God for the Cleveland Indians. If it wasn't for them, we'd be in last place all alone. But instead, because of our win over them today, we've moved up a notch. We're now second to last, while they're the only team in the division that hasn't yet won a game.

It was Guid's first start and win of the year. I hope George takes this one to heart and cools down a little bit. He's been callin' us starting pitchers every name in the book.

Sunday, April 14 — CLEVELAND

Nobody's mother is prouder of her two sons than my mother is of my brother Joe and me. She takes her affection for us real seriously too. In fact, she always carries this lucky umbrella with her wherever she goes. And if someone goes to utterin' a bad word about either Joe or me, she's not afraid to use it. She's already black-and-blued many a fan over the years that have gone to hollerin' bad names at us from the stands.

Mom also likes to hang around outside our clubhouses after the game, when she comes to see us. She's so proud, I guess that it's just her way of gloating. She usually walks up to anybody that looks important and introduces herself. Again, it's just her way of gloating.

I was scheduled to pitch today, so mom and a friend of hers from home drove up to the game today. Whenever she's around, I pitch exceptionally well. I went seven and two-thirds innings, struck out nine, and won my first game of the year. And as usual, after the game mom wanted to hang around outside the clubhouse to introduce herself to the guys as they came out. Since it was the first time she'd seen me play in a Yankee uniform, she was especially anxious. So I arranged it so she could get down there after the game.

Knowing that mom was waiting outside the clubhouse for me, I hurried through my shower and ran out to see her, just in time to catch her walking over to introduce herself to George, who happened to be walking her way.

"Son of a gun," I thought. "Why him, why now?" I just looked down at my mom's lucky umbrella and saw certain disaster appear before my eyes. Hell, George had been blasting us for days. Seeing that there was no way that I could stop the collision, I just turned my head and waited to hear George scream.

But there was no scream. There was no commotion. Mom didn't even raise her umbrella. In fact, as soon as mom walked up and introduced herself to George, George bent down and gave her a big kiss on the cheek and then a big hug. Then he started giving her this shit about how he wished he had twenty-five other players like me. Obviously, he must have sensed that he was in danger and did his best to avoid any sort of conflict.

Then he asked her if there was anything at all he could do for her. She told him that there was, and she requested that a dozen Yankee hats be sent to her home for all my friends and relatives back in Lansing. He assured her that they'd be taken care of the very next day, gave her another big hug and kiss, and then walked away, with all his limbs still firmly attached. One thing you can say about George, he can sure sense when he's overmatched.

Tuesday, April 16 — NEW YORK

If there's one thing that the Cleveland Indians are good for, it's building your confidence. In our home opener today, we battled the White Sox back and forth for almost the entire game, until Don Baylor came up in the ninth, with the score tied 4–4, and declared that he was gonna hit one out.

Hey, Don's a guy with nineteen-inch arms. Whether you believe him or not, for you're own safety it's best just to agree with him. So we all just kinda shook our heads and said, "Yeah, O.K. big guy, get us outta here." But, hell, none of us really knew if he'd do it. I mean, he's big, but he's no damn Babe Ruth.

But he made all of us nonbelievers look like idiots when he took Dan Spillner of the White Sox deep on only his second pitch. It was a solo jobbie but it was all we needed. Dave Righetti, "Rags," got the win after Whit had started but was yanked after six and two-thirds.

The win moved us even farther out of the basement. In fact, Toronto and the Indians are now anchoring down the division. Which should supposedly save Yog from being fired, at least until the morning.

Thursday, April 18 — NEW YORK

There was a quote by George in today's sports section describing his feelings about a horse by the name of Eternal Prince that he had just repurchased a portion of the rights of.

"This is a big, strong, good-looking colt," he was quoted as saying. "He has that certain spark of greatness. He's playful, but when he runs, he's all business. He has a lot of fight in him."

As I read that, a light bulb seemed to go on in my head. With a few minor exceptions, that quote seemed almost exactly like the quote he said about me when I was signed. Son of a gun, maybe I'm no more valuable to him than a horse! Damn, they shoot a horse if it breaks its leg. What'll happen to me if I twist an ankle or lose a few starts in a row? I just wish I'd never seen that in the paper today.

We won our fourth game in a row today, which I hope kills all the rumors about Yog bein' fired for awhile. Dennis Rasmussen, a young left-hander, started for us today. Rassy has as good stuff as anyone in the organization. I guess the only thing he has going against him is that since he's so young, he's also very impressionable, which can really hurt you in an environment such as this. But if the front office doesn't mess with him too much, I'm sure he'll be O.K.

Rassy pitched a real good game today, but we just couldn't get him any runs. He went six and a third and only gave up two runs, but both were unearned. Then Rich Bordi was brought in to relieve him, and we finally won the game in the eighth, when Ken Griffey drove in the winning run with a single. Only a few innings before, Griff, who's a terribly underrated outfielder, made the play of the game when he snared Carlton Fisk's line drive to left, quickly wheeled, and threw the ball to Willie Randolph, the cut-off man, who threw to Don Mattingly at first, doubling off the runner and killing a White Sox rally.

Griff, who's batting .348, also made a great ninth-inning catch of a foul fly deep in the corner that otherwise could have made things rather sticky for us.

· · ·

I kinda wondered when we got Dale Berra from the Pirates, during the off-season, how playin' for his dad would affect him. In spring training, it didn't really seem to bother him, and there didn't seem to be any partiality on his dad's part. But so far this season, it's not the idea of playing for his dad that's been botherin' him. It's what the fans say about him playin' for his dad that seems to get to him.

Tonight was just typical of how he's been goin'. He did well at the plate, goin' two for four with one RBI, but he made two errors, both comin' on one play. I think he just let the fans get to him. They were on his ass all game, and by the time it came for him to make that play, they just had him all psyched out.

They just don't like him 'cause they constantly compare him to all the greatness of his father. But the kid's not a bad player. I just wish they'd give him a chance. Or, at least, try to keep from comparing him with what his father did.

Friday, April 19 — NEW YORK

Guid got his first loss of the year today, but he still pitched real well. All that he really gave up was a two-run homer to Julio Franco of the Indians in the first inning, then he shut 'em down the rest of the way.

But we were just unable to score any runs for him, which is unusual for a Yankee team, especially when we're playin' against Cleveland. I think that everybody just has to get used to their place in our lineup. And right now that's pretty tough because we have so many injuries.

Yog had to bat Bobby Meacham in the leadoff slot tonight because Rickey Henderson isn't ready to rejoin us yet. He's still suffering from a bad ankle. Yog put Bonilla at second last night 'cause Willie Randolph is hurt and Omar Moreno and Henry Cotto are splitting the center-field duties. I guess with all our injuries, we're lucky to have won four games in a row. Also, one thing that the front office has got to realize is that with all the changes he makes each off-season, it's almost impossible for us to get off to a fast start because spring training just isn't long enough for all of us to get used to how each other plays.

The Indians started this young leftie named Heaton tonight. He has really good shit. He'll be O.K. once he gets away from Cleveland. Almost everybody prospers after they leave the Indians. Look at the great Yankee teams of the late seventies. They were built on trades with the Indians. The attitude of the entire organization is the only thing that keeps its players from winning. They've got the talent, but they just don't have the attitude to make it work for them. Like I said, this Heaton is gonna be a damn good pitcher.

Saturday, April 20 — NEW YORK

Win No. 286 came relatively easy. But that's not because of my fine pitching performance, but instead because our bats gave me an early four-run lead. If it wasn't for that lead, Lord knows what would have happened today, because I was anything but sparkling.

I guess it's just tough for me to pitch this early in the season. For some reason, I've always been a terrible early season starter. I usually don't get goin' until we get into the thick of the pennant race. I guess I need that extra challenge to spur me on.

Last year was an exception to that rule, though. I was so fired up after bein' released by the Braves that I just felt like I had something to prove. I also wanted to show George and Clyde King that they had made the right decision by taking a chance on me. So I went out there and just pitched my ass off. As a result, I was one of the top winners in the American League in the early season, which got me a nice welcome to New York. But, normally, I'm terrible this early on.

Today was no exception. Still, surprisingly, I won. I pitched five innings, gave up five hits, four walks, but only two runs.

I heard that *Playgirl* magazine offered Tom Seaver $500 to pose in walking shorts. That kinda stuff happens all the time to big leaguers. Look at all the success that Jim Palmer has had with underwear. Me, I'm just waitin' for *Modern Maturity* to call. I hear they're lookin' for famous athletes to model rocking chairs, and who would be better suited than me?

. . .

Rags is pitching real well. I can see that he's gonna be an essential part of this club again, like last year. Last year was his first year in the bullpen, and Yog, who's a real patient guy, did a fine job in bringing him along and building his confidence.

Yog trained Rags to be our stopper. He only brought him in in save situations and lifted him real quick if the other club started jumping on him. Yog's a real baseball man. He knows that a player's main attribute is his confidence. And though it took him approximately half the season to build up Rags' confidence, I'm sure it's gonna pay off for us this season, as it did in the second half of last season, when Rags, after being taken to school a few times in the first half, was just phenomenal.

Already this season, he has four saves, including his save in tonight's game. Hell, that's not a bad ratio 'cause we only have five wins. At that rate, he'll end up with sixty saves.

Sunday, April 21 — NEW YORK

We're just not scoring runs. We get the guys in scoring position but just can't knock 'em in. And as Yog says, "It'll be difficult to start winning unless we stop not scoring runs." Well put, Yog. It couldn't have been said any better.

But either way you say it, it's the truth. We've stranded seventy-seven runners in the last ten games, most of whom were in scoring position. Today was no exception. We had plenty of chances to blow the game wide open but we could never get the key hit to do so.

Instead, we wound up getting shut out by a trio of no-names—Ruhle, Van Ohlen, and Waddell. Though Ruhle started for the Indians, he was fortunate to walk away with the win. We had guys all over the bases against him, but we just couldn't score. Though he didn't allow any runs, he was gone after only four innings.

Then they brought on this kid Van Ohlen, who shut us down completely for the next four before giving way to Waddell, who's Cleveland's version of the Goose and came in and hurled one inning for his third save of the year.

Already, this year is beginning to look a lot like last year.

We're makin' the same mistakes and gettin' beaten by teams that shouldn't be beating us. I really think that if George weren't so interested in his new play toy, Eternal Prince, which he just sank over two million dollars into, there'd be a whole lot more hell to pay around here.

George is kinda hopin' that the horse is gonna win the Derby this year. I'm kinda hopin' it will too, 'cause that'll keep him off our backs even longer. But if the sucker loses, there'll be hell to pay. And I have this sneaky feeling that we'll be the ones who'll have to pay it.

George finally came out and admitted in the newspaper today that he prefers thoroughbreds to baseball players. Why? Because thoroughbreds don't talk to sportswriters.

Whit started today. He's been a hardluck pitcher so far this season. For the second start in a row, he turned in a decent outing. With the lineup that we have, that usually translates into a win. But not today. In fact, we've been outscored 21–10 in games in which Whit has started. I know that a lot of that may have to do with how he's been pitchin'; but, heck, we should be able to get the score at least a little closer than that.

As a result, he's pushing a little too much. He just wants that first victory so bad. Also, with the money George is payin' him, I think he believes that he's supposed to become the ace of the staff or somethin'. Hell, he's just gotta keep in mind that if George hadn't given the money away to him he would've just found somebody else to give it away to.

Monday, April 22, OFF DAY—NEW YORK

Yog defines a voluntary workout as meaning that "you don't have to come." So since we hadn't had an off-day yet this season and since most of us needed to get our shit together as far as living conditions and such were concerned, nearly all of us took advantage of Yog's generosity and took the day off. Which really ticked off George.

At the beginning of the day, it appeared that the workout had been staged solely to introduce Rickey Henderson to New York, since he had joined the team for the first time this season and was scheduled to be at the stadium working out today. But when he came out of the clubhouse and totally ignored the press until after he was finished working out, Safety had to do something with the media to entertain them. So he took them up to George's box for an impromptu press conference, one which George used to express his dissatisfaction concerning the small number of players at the workout. He started quoting Vince Lombardi and all that shit. He must be really mad, 'cause then and only then does he quote Lombardi, his idol.

Tuesday, April 23 — NEW YORK

The press has been billing our three-game series with the Red Sox as the BRAWL IN THE BRONX. That's how George sees it anyway. He's got Yog doin' commercials promoting it and everything. I even think that George's main purpose in having Rickey rejoin the team is so that he'd be ready for this series. George just hates losing to the Red Sox worse than losing to anybody but the Mets.

But brawl or no brawl, we only drew 25,000 and got beat again by the Red Sox, our fifth loss in a row to them this season. We just looked bad. It was Hendy's first game as a Yankee, and I think the fans were expecting a little bit too much, especially with the guy still nursing an extremely sore ankle. They booed New York's supposedly soon-to-be-favorite son when he lined into an inning-ending double play, with the score tied in the eighth, and then lined out to center with the tying run on second, in the eleventh.

Boston finally won the game in the eleventh, when they scored a run off of Rags. All in all, though, we were poor. We committed a total of four errors on the day, not including several mental errors, and again were unable to get that key hit to break the game wide open. Our lackluster performance caused George to remark sarcastically, "Oh, no, this team didn't need a workout."

In fact, George was so pissed off after the game that he totally lost control. He started quoting Vince Lombardi again, a man who believed in discipline in its truest form, and even admitted that he had contacted Earl Weaver about managing the club after our opening-season massacre in Boston.

Right now, it does not look good for Yog.

Wednesday, April 24 — NEW YORK

Our loss today dropped us into last place, yes, even below the Indians, and may have put Yog in the unemployment line. Again, we just played like shit. Hendy, who just hasn't gotten used to his new environment yet, again was a little shaky. It was his first-inning error that opened the doors for Boston. And it was Griff's error later that inning that continued to hold the doors open, as the Red Sox scored four runs off of Guid, who was pitching reasonably well.

Though we fought back to tie the score at six before the Red Sox came back and won it on Jim Rice's solo homer in the seventh, George is still really pissed, still harping on Yog's decision to go with a "voluntary" workout last Monday.

"You can't tell me this team doesn't need a workout," he said. "Look at them, they're killing me."

It seems now that whether or not Yog keeps his job all comes down to whether George is able to digest the fact that Yog didn't hold a mandatory workout on Monday. Unless, of course, we can put together a string of wins *reeaaalll* quick.

I'm starting to believe that this shit about a brawl with the Red Sox is gonna come to life. They've got a real young pitching staff, one that isn't afraid to throw at guys. In fact, that's how they make up for their lack of talent and experience, by buzzing guys.

But these guys gotta be loaded with stupidity, too. Hell, you don't go buzzing the Dave Winfields and Don Baylors. Guys like that'll tear your damn head off. If ya throw at anybody, you pick either a batter that's a lot smaller than you or one that you can outrun.

Tonight, Baylor was buzzed by Al Nipper in the second and

had to be restrained by the home-plate ump. Then in the fifth, Baylor was again knocked down, this time by Steve Crawford, causing both benches to empty, as Baylor stood there just glaring at Crawford.

I don't think George can say that we're not playin' with any intensity. He should have seen the look in Baylor's eyes tonight. It was even more frightening then the sight of his nineteen-inch arms.

He can say that we're playing awful, which isn't anyone's fault but our own, and certainly not Yog's. But he can't say that we aren't playing with intensity, which is the key ingredient to overcoming our mistakes in the long run. I wish he'd just be patient and wait until we all get our shit together, especially for Yog's sake, who's a damn good manager. Just give him time, George. We'll be O.K.

Thursday, April 25 — NEW YORK

Maury Allen wrote a satirical article in the *Post* today making fun of George's love for horse racing, listing the odds-on favorites to replace Yog as the new Yankee manager.

Allen's list was headed by Billy Martin, at 4–1, and ran all the way down to Hank Steinbrenner, George's son, at 150–1.

I don't know about George's son, though. I just can't see George hiring someone that he wouldn't be able to fire. Well, but then again. He's only George's son.

When I got to the clubhouse, around three o'clock this afternoon, it was already filled with reporters, and I just kinda figured that it was over, that Yog had been fired. I was very surprised to find out that he was still here. "George must just be having a hard time convincing Hank to take the job," I thought.

Then I realized the true importance of our game tonight. Not only were we trying to win just for ourselves, but mostly for Yog. If we dropped another one to the Red Sox, which would be our sixth in a row this season, there would be no way for George to face the media without firing Yog. We all knew that, we all liked Yog, and none of us wanted to see him go.

Fortunately, after having beaten Cleveland twice in a row, I was in a groove and turned in my finest performance of the year. As I waited on the mound in the eighth inning for Yog to walk out and relieve me, Yog's kid, Dale, just kept slapping me on the arm saying, "Great game Phil. Great fuckin' game." Shit, my arm hurt more from Little Yog's continual slapping of it than it did from pitchin' my seven and two thirds.

When Yog got to the mound, he took the ball from me and told me to head in.

"No, that's O.K., Yog," I said, "I'll wait for Rags."

Yog just looked so exhausted. Even earlier in the day, Yog had done something totally uncharacteristic by losing his temper and telling a reporter that the only thing he still liked about his job was the game. An obvious slap at George.

I really felt for the man. He'd been under a tremendous amount of pressure over the last few weeks. And for what? For something that not even he had the power to control. I just kinda hung around waitin' for Rags so I could walk in with Yog, kinda of a show of solidarity, a way of showing that not only I, but all the other guys, were behind him.

As I walked off the mound, Yog followed approximately six feet behind and a group of fans behind our dugout stood up and applauded. Though I knew the ovation was more for Yog than me, I still felt good because I knew that I had done what I had set out to do that day, and that Yog would have been our manager for at least one more day because of it.

Friday, April 26 — CHICAGO

I think we're all trying too hard, feelin' the pressure too much. We feel like every time one of us comes to the plate, it's a crucial at-bat. We left fourteen guys on base again tonight. And, again, Whit was the victim. He's becoming totally frustrated.

He took a no-hitter into the fifth but then gave up a three-run homer to Harold Baines, which gave the White Sox a lead they would never lose. Though we had guys on base all night, we just couldn't score and wound up losing 4–2. We're just tryin' too hard, all of us, Yog included. He's no longer his usual friendly self. He's tense, taut, worried. He knows that his job may hang on the basis of one wrong move. It's a terrible type of environment to be a part of, even a worse one to play in.

I think that all that kept Yog from being fired today was the fact that George was in Kentucky tending to the needs of his new horse, who was scheduled to race tomorrow. He's just too busy with that right now to take any definite action on the situation. Which may serve as a blessing and give us at least one more day to break out of this slump and change his mind.

Saturday, April 27 — CHICAGO

We were the NBC Game of the Week, so George got to see us play today while also getting to see his horse run. Although it would have probably been better for all concerned if the game had been blacked out.

Though we took an early 3–0 lead, the White Sox scored two in the bottom of the ninth to tie the score and take the game into extra innings. Yog was just not at his best today. In fact, his nerves were fuckin' shattered. The constant pressure had finally gotten to him. It was his mismoves that led to the White Sox' tying of the game—and to their eventual victory.

It almost seemed as if he subconsciously wanted to lose the game, just to get all this shit over with. He always seemed to pull the exact wrong move at the right time, or bring in the exact wrong pitcher for a situation. I felt sorry for him 'cause he's under so much pressure that he can't even think.

Though we went ahead 4–3, with a run in the top of the eleventh, it was a series of Yog's decisions that led to the White Sox scoring two runs in the bottom of the eleventh, and thus to our 5–4 loss.

Sunday, April 28 — CHICAGO

Today, it finally happened, and in fitting fashion. Yog was fired after our 4–3 loss to the White Sox, a game in which Chicago scored in the bottom of the ninth to win it. Supposedly, George had made his decision after watching his horse run yesterday and then watching us falter—a terribly unfair comparison between a championship horse and a confused baseball team. I guess I should just feel fortunate that George didn't decide to get rid of all of us.

Nobody liked the move, but we all knew it was comin'. But even yet, most of us found it difficult to control our emotions. Donny Mattingly, who's a real Yogi man, just started screaming at the top of his lungs and throwing trash cans, or anything he could get his hands on, across the room. Other guys just sat around in disbelief. They just couldn't believe that it had happened. We just couldn't believe that Yog had been fired only sixteen games into the season.

Then when it was announced that Billy Martin had been named to take Yog's place, the clubhouse took on a totally new complexion, one of anger. I guess most of the guys around here just don't like ol' Billy.

Baylor, who's our team captain, sensed that things were startin' to get out of control, so he started shooing the reporters out of the clubhouse, and all of them left without any hassle, except this one black guy, who started to give Baylor some shit. Which was the wrong fuckin' thing to do at this time.

Baylor, who dislikes Martin worse than probably anyone, tried to remain cordial and polite, but the guy just kept raggin' on Baylor's ass about constitutional rights and shit. So Don started chasin' the little son of a gun out of the clubhouse. Then the guy had the balls to slam the door right in Don's face.

Baylor tore the damn door right off its hinges. It took ten of us to hold him back. He wanted to kill the little shit.

After everything calmed back down, Yog came around to each one of us, shook our hands and wished us luck. He's such a class act. There was a look of relief on his face, a look of calm that I hadn't seen there before.

Though I believe that his firing was totally unfair and that the abuse that he had to take was way too extensive, I do believe that it was the best thing for both Yog and the club at this time. George may do things half ass-backwards at times, but he's still intent on winning and bringing a winner to New York, and he'll do whatever it takes to do so, including firing the most popular manager in the club's history.

Monday, April 29, 1985 — TEXAS

Yog was fired yesterday, and I didn't really know what to think about the re-re-re-rehiring of Billy Martin 'cause I don't like to judge a guy by what I've heard or read about him. Especially in Martin's case. Shit, if his mother had read all that I'd read on him and heard what I'd heard, even she'd probably have a hard time likin' him. Charles Manson would've looked good next to him. So I just kinda decided to keep quiet and outta sight the first few days, to see what kinda guy this Billy Martin really was—before I had any type of run-in with him. All I hoped was that Billy Martin was nothin' like the reputation that preceded him, that of the Great Slayer of the Marshmallow Salesman.

On the flight here last night I had tried to get an idea from some of the guys who had played for him before on what type of guy he really was, and the reviews came out kinda mixed. But the majority of the guys refused to say anything at all for fear of losing control. Especially Don Mattingly, who loved Yog like a father. Donny says that he's gonna wear his Yogi Berra "It Ain't Over 'Till It's Over" T-shirt under his jersey for the rest of the season in silent tribute.

Nobody would really come out and say that they loved Martin. In fact, nobody would even admit to liking him. About the closest anybody would come was Rickey Henderson, who started his career under Martin in Oakland. But then Hendy wasn't even that complimentary. All he said was, "Billy's an all right guy." Which isn't very much for a guy to say about the manager who gave him a chance to play in the big leagues, and about a manager who helped nurture him into the million-dollar-a-year star he has become.

I guess Willie Randolph summed it up best when he said, "You just won't believe it around here after Billy gets here. You thought things were crazy, well they're gonna get really crazy now. You ain't seen nothin' yet!"

After running Willie's description through my mind about a thousand times today and bein' the kind of laid back guy that I am, I decided just to try and blend into the background today, hopin' to hold off meeting ol' Billy Martin as long as possible.

So I just disguised myself as your typical forty-six-year-old, half-naked, big-league knuckleball pitcher.

But about an hour before game time, Martin happened to catch me strolling across the clubhouse and called me over. All I could think to myself was, "What the hell? Why me? Why the hell today?"

I can just see it now, my bust mounted right along side that of that marshmallow salesman in Martin's den, like two damn prize water buffalos or somethin'. I can just see it in tomorrow's *Post*: MARTIN BAGS 46-YEAR-OLD PITCHER. Why me? Why today?

When I got over to him, I kinda kept my head down to guard against the right hook. But he surprised me. Without even a handshake or any type of introduction, he started right in, "What do you think of Bonilla?"

"What?" I asked myself. What the hell is he asking me that for? Must be some type of deceptive move to get me off balance. Yeah, but I won't fall for that shit. I'll just answer his question like I don't even know what he's tryin' to do.

"Well, I don't know," I responded hesitantly. "He's a good little play . . ."

But before I even got a chance to finish, he fired back, "Fuckin' gone! Fuckin' gone, Niekro! I'm bringin' up Hudler."

I thought to myself, this is a real strange way to start a fight. He's deceptive. He must be trying to get me off balance or somethin'. Well, then, maybe he thought that Juan and I were real close friends or somethin' and he was just tryin' to fool with me by gettin' rid of him right in front of me. But, hell, Bonilla and I didn't even speak the same language. I wonder what tactic he used to rope that marshmallow salesman into duelin' with him?

He must have thought what he had said to me was real funny 'cause it took him quite a while before he stopped laughing long enough to ask me, "What about Fisher? Whattya think about him?"

Obviously, he was having a really damn good time because right after he asked me that he broke into laughter again. I felt like a stooge on candid camera or somethin'. Maybe George was filmin' this whole thing and was gonna play it back for his wife and kids, just for kicks.

Still leery of his right hook, I replied, "The guy's got a great arm, but he's known for being a little wild at times."

"But you think he can pitch?" he fired back.

"Yeah, he can pitch, but he's gonna walk a few guys and hit a few, too." That seemed to stop him in his tracks. Why, I don't know, but it did, and a sly, serious smile appeared on his face. He had obviously liked something that I said about Fisher, but what I don't know.

"Hey, there's nothin' wrong with walkin' a few guys, is there?"

"No, *welllll*, I guess not."

"He'll be fuckin' here tomorrow," he said before turning away, having accomplished his task. No, I guess I haven't seen nothin' yet.

We're playin' really bad, no matter who the manager is this week. Tonight, Bobby Meacham hit what would have been a three-run homer and passed Willie on the bases and turned it into a two-run single.

I just kept lookin' over at Martin, waitin' and waitin' for him to erupt, knowing that my quick reactions may be all that could stand between Meach, Martin, and a broken jaw for Meach. But no punch, no screams, not even a squeak from Martin. This was obviously not the Billy Martin that I had read and heard so many wonderful things about.

Then just a few minutes later, John "the Count" Montefusco, who Martin had activated just before the game, hung a 1–0 curveball to Larry Parish, who hit it out for his third homer of the game. And still nothin' from Martin. Could this be a sane impostor that we were dealing with and not the tyrannical Billy Martin we had heard so much about?

Tuesday, April 30 — TEXAS

I was gettin beat around pretty bad tonight, but I'd been pretty lucky. The Rangers had only scored five runs off me in the first four innings.

Then in the fifth, the Rangers got a few guys on, and Billy came out to the mound.

"Knock the next son of a bitch on his ass," he said, then scurried back to the dugout.

As he ran back, I glanced up at the scout behind home plate, who normally gauges the speed of our pitchers with a radar gun. But with me, he was using an egg timer.

"Shit," I said to myself. "What the hell is buzzin' a guy with a sixty-five mile per hour knuckleball gonna prove? We're only down by one run, and to risk puttin' another guy on base would be stupid."

I just couldn't understand what he was thinkin'. I mean, it just didn't make sense. But then I got to thinkin' that maybe this was another one of Martin's tactics to get a fight started. He couldn't entice me yesterday, even after insulting Bonilla, so he decided to try using this method today.

But then I began to remember his clubhouse meeting yesterday, the first one I ever remember in all my years in the big leagues being almost totally devoted to knocking guys down.

"I don't want ya to hurt anybody, but then *uuuummmmmmm*, when I tell ya to knock somebody down, ya better do so or it's gonna cost ya a grand."

Shit, I'd knock my own mother down to win a game. So I came up and in with my blazing sixty-five mile per hour hummer. Intimidation at its best! The guy ended up gettin' a hit off me on the very next pitch. Damn intimidating!

A little later in the game, I don't know why, but somehow I was still in the damn game, and we're now down 7–3 and Cliff Johnson comes to the plate. Now, Johnson had already hit the ball hard off me twice, but I went and got ahead of him real quick with two knucklers, 0–2.

On the next pitch, I decided to loosen him up a bit, move him off the plate a little, so I came up high and inside with my hummer and he just kinda looked at me and laughed, as if to say, "You old shit, what the hell are you tryin' to do?" Which really pissed me off, 'cause no one likes to be shown up.

So the next day I'm sittin' on the bench before the game ,and Johnson, who's takin' batting practice, yells over at me, "Hey, you old goat! What do you think you're doin' comin' up and in on me like that?"

Now that really pissed me off, 'cause now he was showin' me up in front of all my teammates.

"What the hell were you laughin' at?" I asked.

"What do you expect me to do when you're throwing that weak shit up there like that?"

I just looked him straight in the eye and said, "Next time you laugh at me, I'm gonna knuckle one right up your ass."

Hudler was called up. He'll primarily be used as a back-up infielder. Actually, his best position is second base, but it used to be shortstop until George saw him play a game in which he committed two errors and ordered that he never be allowed to play short again.

Billy's making a lot of moves already. Tonight, he flip-flopped Winnie and Don in the lineup, Winnie to clean-up and Don to the third spot, but we still lost our fifth straight. One more loss and Billy might be outta here.

I can just see it now—a new manager for every week of the season. Or how about if we started havin' celebrity guest managers, like they do with game shows. Then the team would really take on a personality all its own; yeah, like a multiple personality.

Wednesday, May 1—TEXAS

Billy was a little upset after we lost last night, but not the kind of upset I expected him to be. He didn't scream at anybody, didn't throw anything and didn't hit anyone. All he did was skip going downstairs to the hotel bar for a few drinks after the game. The Billy Martin that I've heard so much about would've never skipped a chance to have a few drinks after a game. This guy we've got managing our club has to be an impostor!

Tonight, Billy used Omar Moreno in right field instead of Winnie, and put Ron Hassey in as the DH. Billy wants to win this one real bad, and he thought that Charlie Hough's knuckleball would really screw up Winnie and Don Baylor, who are really struggling, even worse if he left them in there.

The changes seemed to help, especially putting Hass in as DH, 'cause he had four hits and drove in four runs, both of which were probably single-game career highs for him. Hey, for a guy who's spent the majority of his career in Cleveland, what do you want?

Whit started tonight and was horseshit. That's why Billy was so quick to bring in Rags Righetti tonight. He didn't want to lose this one and wind up with the same fate as his old buddy Yogi.

Rags pitched four innings of one-hit relief and got the first win of the season for both Whit and Billy. For obvious reasons, Billy just wanted this one real bad.

Slowly Billy is making this club into his type of team. One thing you can say about the guy, he isn't afraid to make changes. And, surprisingly, he hasn't offended anyone with one yet.

Rumor has it that he is gonna do somethin' with Jeff Torborg though. Torborg is a real Yogi guy. What Billy'll do only time will tell. And how Billy'll use him, I don't know.

Dale Berra fractured a finger on his dad's last day. He isn't playin' so he just spends the majority of his time walkin' around the clubhouse askin' everybody, "My dad was an O.K. guy wasn't he? I mean, he was easy to play for, right? I mean ya liked him, didn't ya?"

Hey, I feel sorry for the kid. I know he loves his dad and all, and I'd probably feel the same way if it had been my dad.

Friday, May 3 — NEW YORK

I kept a pretty close eye on Billy today. I just couldn't believe that this was the same guy that was so notorious for kicking dirt on the shoes of umpires and slugging marshmallow salesmen.

In fact, he's one of the nicest guys I've ever met. He's great with the media. Hell, today a swarm of 'em were all around him, and he took time to talk to each one. He didn't cuss anybody out or insult any female reporters or call them sluts or anything.

When he wasn't with the media, he just walked around the

clubhouse jokin' with all the guys. Hell, we've lost two out of the last three, and from what I've heard he isn't supposed to be like this at all, especially when the team is playing as bad as we are.

This is just not the Billy Martin that I've heard so many bad things about. I just can't understand how everybody could have been so wrong about this guy.

The guys that have been around Billy before are now saying that we're playing Billyball. I don't know what the hell that is, but I do know that we're playin' more aggressive baseball. Billy's got the guys stealing, hittin' and running, moving baserunners along. He's really getting things flowin' and the guys seem to be havin' more fun now, too.

We won tonight, 7–1, which is the most runs we've scored all season. Rassy pitched a complete game. It was the best I've seen him pitch this season. Now all Billy has to do is get the front office to stay off Rassy's ass so his concentration can grow. He's got all the tools to be an outstanding pitcher, but he's still a little bit unsure of himself. Some nights he goes out there and looks like Cy Young and other nights you wonder if he'll even be able to get anyone out. But if they leave him alone, he'll be O.K. And for our sake, I hope they do, 'cause we can sure use another starting pitcher.

Billyball ran us into a triple play tonight, but it was an aggressive mistake, not a stupid mistake, which makes it O.K.

Oddly, Rickey Henderson, easily the fastest guy on the team, hit into it. It happened in the sixth, with Billy Sample on second and Meach on first. Billy sent the runners and Hendy lined a soft liner to Frank White at second. It was a mistake, but it was an aggressive mistake. And without aggressiveness, there would have been no way that we could have scored runs tonight.

I'm just glad for Billy's sake that it happened on the eve of the Kentucky Derby. 'Cause if George hadn't been so concerned with his horse running, Billy may have been gone and somebody like Don Rickles a real take charge guy, may have been in. And I'd also hate to see a guy like Billy get fired.

. . .

Torborg was moved outta the bullpen today and put on first base. It almost seems like a promotion. Maybe all the rumors about Torburg being on the outs were wrong, 'cause Martin just doesn't seem like the kind of guy who would just get rid of the guy. As far as I'm concerned, he's proved his critics wrong again.

We had a Derby pool today. The names of all the horses were put in a hat, and for $20 you got to choose a slip of paper with a name of one of the horses on it out of the hat. Then the money was divided among the guys holding the top three finishers.

Dale picked George's horse, Eternal Prince. We all agreed that because of that the boy was doomed for some certain disaster. He's probably gonna be our next manager. Just think, Dale could be the first manager in baseball ever to replace the man who replaced his father.

Saturday, May 4 — NEW YORK

Guid pitched tonight like the Ron Guidry of old. Not so much that he was overpowering, but he was in total control of his game.

Last year, Guid changed from a straight power pitcher to a part-time finesse pitcher who can still blow it by ya if he has to, but simply just not as frequently as before. As a result of his change, he had the worst year of his career last year—yet a year that a lotta guys would have been happy to have. So there were a lotta so called baseball experts around that said that Guid had had it, he was washed up. Shows ya how much they know.

Hell, all great pitchers that stick around for any length of time have to go through some type of change to accommodate their advancing age. And when they do, they usually have a year like Guid did last year. Look at Seaver, Gaylord Perry, me. Heck, those two guys adjusted their styles to compensate for their advancing years. They went from primarily fastball pitchers to finesse pitchers.

Look at me, I went from a slow-ball pitcher to an even slower pitcher, and I survived. Besides about ten years and thirty miles per hour on our fastballs, what's the big difference between Guid and me?

Thank God Guid's back, 'cause we need him real bad. 'Cause right now I'm about the only starter who's pitching with any type of consistency.

I just can't believe it! After the game today, I heard that Torborg was gonna be fired. Right from the bullpen to first base to gone in a matter of six days—or FUCKIN' GONE! as Billy would have put it.

Well, maybe I've been wrong about Billy. But I just can't figure out how such a nice guy could be so deceptive and misleading. *Nnnnooooooo*, someone else must have gotten involved, like George. I just can't see it coming from Billy, especially after the guy had only been at his new position for one game.

So what that the team ran into a triple play. He was given only one night to prove himself? Unless, of course, Billy set him up. Naw, not a guy as nice as Billy. No way he would ever do that to someone.

Sunday, May 5 — NEW YORK

When I got to the park today, there was a group of tough-looking, war-torn GI's hanging around outside the stadium and the first thing I thought was, "Ah, shit, Billy's been fired and George hired these mercenaries to hold back the rioting crowds. Shit, right in the middle of a winning streak, a small winning streak, but a winning streak nonetheless."

But after I got in the clubhouse and started asking around, I found out that the guys were just part of a group of Vietnam Vets who were marching across the country and who George invited to the game once they got to New York.

I didn't have squat today, but I won No. 288, thanks to our bats and a bad wager by Dale Berra.

When I was warming up before the game, I could see that I was gonna have a tough day of it, no knuckleball. But the guys were swinging real well and supported me with four homers.

But the key play of the game came in the fifth inning when

Little Yog led off with a single. At the time the game was tied, 1–1.

Billy Sample was the next batter. And Martin, looking to stay out of the double play, called for a hit-and-run, and Sample grounded sharply to third. At first, it looked like an easy double play.

George Brett wheeled and fired to second, but just as the ball got there, Yog, who was still fuckin' incensed at losing $20 in the Derby pool (and of all horses, he lost it on George's), took out his aggressions on poor, innocent Frank White at second, sending the Royal second sacker sprawling across the infield, and breaking up the potential double play. Which eventually set the stage for Rickey Henderson's two-run homer, which won the game for us.

We wound up winning 6–2. I struggled for seven and a third innings and had absolutely nothin' but my old reliable sixty-five mile per hour fastball. I ended up walking six. Win No. 288—that's the first time I ever won a game via the outcome of a Derby pool.

Tuesday, May 7— MINNESOTA

When they first turn on the lights in this damn place, they're blinding. It's the only place in baseball where your guys have to wear sunglasses for a night game. Christ, we all look like Stevie Wonders out there.

The lights for the first few innings are just unbearable. You take one damn look at them without adequate eye protection, and you're blinded until the next equinox.

Here you should be allowed to have a designated ground ball pitcher to start every game until the lights cool down, just to save your players' eyes. Shit, after a long home stand, I bet the Twins all look like albinos.

Tonight, we lost two or three routine pop-ups in just the first two innings. I mean, like Whit really needs any help giving up runs with the way he's been pitching. He wound up giving up five in the first one and two thirds, then his ass was gone and we wound up losing, 8–6.

Roy Smalley, one of those guys that George trades for, signs to a big contract, trades away while still having to pay off most of his contract, and who then comes back to haunt the Yanks, did just that tonight. Guys like this just love to come back and do this to old George, 'cause they know that it pisses him off so, and nothin' makes a former Yankee happier than that. Tonight, he did it not only with his bat, which he is famous for, but also with his glove, which he is infamous for amongst New York fans. Just a little more salt in the wound for old George and the Yanks.

Griff wants outta here real bad. Today, he called Clyde King and asked him to trade him to a National League club.

Griff was also one of the guys who wasn't too crazy about Billy's re-re-re-rehiring. Supposedly, Griff had some kind of scuffle with Billy a few years ago over having his kids visit him in the clubhouse. But I guess Griff had a difficult time accepting Billy's ways and just never got over their scuffle. There's a lot of people who never get over having a scuffle with Billy; just ask that marshmallow salesman from Minneapolis.

Griff just couldn't hold it in anymore after Billy decided to start platooning him with Billy Sample, who hit his first homer for us on Sunday and who is a real dedicated guy. Hell, just the other day, Billy shaved off his mustache after going zero for four. We told him today that if he was slumping as bad as Griff, it'd only be a few more days before he'd be shaving his balls.

I still haven't seen that bad side of Billy that everyone keeps talkin' about. In fact, he seems to have a pretty good sense of humor. Last weekend a reporter asked him why he hadn't decorated his office at Yankee Stadium yet. Billy replied: "I think I'll leave it like this. 'Cause every time I get it lookin' pretty, I ain't here anymore." Now does that sound like the fanatical maniac that you hear so much about?

Wednesday, May 8 — MINNESOTA

Billy went berserk today. The real Billy Martin must be back. Hell, he protested today's game even before it began.

And George got right into it, too, by issuing an official statement this afternoon that in a nice way stated that the Metrodump was a horseshit place to play in. It's good to see two friends that have been so close for so long still getting along so well.

Protest or no protest, Joe Cowley started for us tonight and was horseshit. He's just all messed up. After having been buried in Atlanta's farm system for so long, I think Joe hoped he'd finally get a fair shake here, which he did, until now, that is.

He initially joined us from Columbus about halfway through last season. At first, Yog had him stationed in the bullpen. But then we needed an extra starter, so Yog gave Joe a chance and he responded with eight wins in nine starts. In fact, during that time, I thought he was the best pitcher in the American League, if not all of baseball. And if there was one player who was responsible for our resurgence in the second half, it was Joe.

But during the off-season, the Yanks traded Jay Howell, who was Rag's set-up guy, to the A's in the Henderson deal, and somebody got the bright idea that Cowls would be the perfect guy to replace him. So in spring training, Joe, our best starter in the second half of last season, was converted back into a reliever, which really burst the kid's bubble.

As a result, he had a terrible spring and has been just as bad so far this season. I just can't understand how someone would fool with a potential eighteen-to-twenty-game winner, especially when we don't have that many quality starters as it is. Whatever, it really blew his mind. It just didn't make sense to him, which would be a normal reaction in this circumstance.

So when he took the mound tonight, he was extremely confused, at best. He didn't know if he was a starter or a reliever and he was real nervous, pitching for Billy for the first time and all.

As a result, he looked bad, real bad! He gave up seven runs in three and two-thirds innings and dropped to 0–2 on the season, as we lost by a score of 8–6.

Thursday, May 9, OFF DAY—KANSAS CITY

Joe was sent down to Columbus today and John Montefusco was retrieved from the disabled list.

Friday, May 10 — KANSAS CITY

Dominic Scala is our bullpen catcher and one of the funniest guys I've ever met, Uecker included. Dom doesn't even have to say anything to make me laugh, just standing there is enough.

Dom is a dreamer, a guy who constantly dreams of becoming a big leaguer. He isn't satisfied with his role as our bullpen catcher, even though he travels with us and is treated like a big leaguer. No, sir, Dom wants to be an honest-to-God big leaguer. But at his age—he's in his mid-thirties—and with his degree of talent, the chances of his dream ever coming true seem almost impossible. And the guys know that, so they're on his shit all the time, raggin' him about becomin' a big leaguer or jaggin' him about being a horseshit catcher.

But Dom takes all the ribbin' pretty well. Hell, he's been in the big leagues almost ten years, ever since whoever was the back-up catcher at that time refused to warm up any pitchers and George went hunting for a bullpen catcher and bagged Dom, right out of Class A ball.

The other day Dom came up to me and told me a story, one of the funniest ones I ever heard and one that he would swear on a stack of rosary beads is true.

It seems that on the last home stand, Dom was standing around in the bullpen after havin' warmed up that night's starter doin' basically nothin', except maybe pickin' his nose, when this guy starts hollerin' down at him, actually callin' him by name, from the charity section out in the bleachers. Dom was shocked. Hell, someone actually knew him. Heck, just like being a big leaguer.

Playin' it to the hilt, Dom just walked over to the guy, who was motioning him over to the rail, real slow like he had something very important on his mind, like how he was gonna have his pitcher pitch to George Brett that evening or somethin'. So when Dom finally got over to the guy, the guy was nearly in hysterics. Dom thought to himself. "The guy just must really want my autograph."

So Dom held out his hand, waiting for the guy to either shake it vigorously or place a pen in it for him to sign a ball, bat, or the guy's forehead or somethin. But the guy did neither. Instead, he just started beggin' Dom to watch a section full of retarded kids he brought to the game while he ran to the men's room and took a shit.

"Hey, if I don't get there real damn fast I'm gonna bust," the guy said.

"And they're only damn derelicts," he continued. "They don't know nothin' and they won't be any trouble."

Somewhat disappointed that the guy didn't ask for his autograph but yet feelin' real compassionate toward the guy's situation, Dom said that he'd help him out but wanted to know what he had to do.

"Well, when they play the national anthem," the guy began, "You just tell 'em to stand up by motionin' your arms up like this and sayin', 'Stand up, nuts, stand up.' Then when the anthem is over, all ya do is motion your arms downward like this and say, 'Sit down, nuts, sit down,' and the damn derelicts will sit down. It's as easy as that. And by the time the anthem is over, I'll be back from the crapper and you can go back to doin' whatever it is that you do."

Dom, still a little disappointed, hesitantly shook his head in agreement and the guy was gone in a flash, runnin' up the stairs to the men's room like his life depended on it. Well, then, maybe by that point it did.

So when the announcer asked all the fans to stand for the playing of the national anthem, Dom did just as the guy had told him to do. He motioned upwards with his arms, just as the guy had said, and said, "Stand up, nuts, stand up," and the kids did just as he asked. Then when the anthem was over, Dom again did just as the guy said, motioning downward and sayin', "Sit down, nuts, sit down."

And only a few minutes later the guy was back from the men's room, just as he had promised. But by this time all the nuts were standing up, grabbin' their crotches, and holdin' their noses and the guy went berserk, jumpin' all over Dom about what happened.

In defense of himself Dom said, "I did just as you told me: 'Stand up, nuts, stand up,' and 'Sit down, nuts, sit down,' and all that shit. And everything went just fine until some goddamn vendor came by yelling, '*Peeaannuuttss, Peeeaaannnnuuutttsss!*' "

Guid was great tonight, as he got his third win and Rags came in and shut the door on the last two innings for his eighth save, as we won, 6–4.

Saturday, May 11—KANSAS CITY

We beat Kansas City for the tenth time in a row tonight. They haven't beaten us since the "Great Pine Tar" incident. I just don't think that they've been able to convince themselves that that actually happened. Hell, it's real laid back and calm down here in ol' Kansas City, and I think that incident kinda knocked their socks off. Shit, but if they had been playin' here in New York instead of in Kansas City, that wouldn't have even bothered 'em. That type of shit happens around here about every other minute.

Rassy pitched another good game tonight. He might be that extra starter that we need. Billy gave this kid Brian Fisher a chance to finish up and he did real well. Billy really likes the kid, especially the fact that the kid has a "slightly wild" ninety-five mile per hour fastball. He's Billy's type of pitcher. He always keeps the batters guessin', guessin' whether they're gonna be able to walk away from the plate after facin' him or not.

Fish's type of intimidation kinda reminds me of how Bob Veale, of the Pirates, used to go after hitters. Like Fish, he had a "slightly wild" blazing fastball that just scared the hell out of hitters. But it kept 'em honest.

In fact, in one game, Veale somehow broke his glasses and didn't have a second pair so he just decided to go ahead and keep pitching anyway, which was O.K. with his manager, O.K. with the umpire, but not O.K. with the hitters. Hell, Bob had a hard time findin' the plate when he could see it clearly. Without his glasses, he actually stood a better chance of hitting the batter, who was a bigger target, than crossin' the plate with a strike.

And that's how Lou Brock, of the Cardinals, one of the smartest guys to ever play the game, saw it. He refused to even step in against Bobby. That's why I think ol' Lou was one of the smartest guys ever to play the game.

Today, mom called me and she sounded a little irritated and a lost confused, and I asked her what was the matter. She told me that she hadn't gotten her hats yet from "Mr. Steinbrenner," and she wondered if she should call him about it.

"Hell, yeah, you should call him," I said.

"You sure he's gonna remember me?" she asked.

"Sure he is," I responded. "Just tell him that you're the lady who's gonna transform him into a soprano if you don't get your goddamn hats real fast."

Sunday, May 12 — KANSAS CITY

Like all good businessmen, Lou Piniella knows how to take advantage of a good opportunity. They're just crazy about him here in Kansas City; that's why he decided to open up a restaurant/bar downtown.

While we've been in town, a few of the guys went down to visit the place. Two of 'em, Yog and Donny, got arrested. The arresting officers called it indecent conduct, which I feel is totally a judgment call. In fact, in the case of Yog, I think he should almost consider that a compliment.

I guess that what happened is that Donny went down there at night on our off-day, on Thursday, to have a few drinks and a little somethin' to eat. When he started walking back to the hotel, he had to take a leak, so he snuck around behind a dumpster and did just so. Unfortunately, a few patrolling policemen caught him in the act and arrested him.

Then, on Saturday, Yog, who's not much for learning from the mistakes of others, went down to Lou's place, too. And like Donny, on the way home had to take a piss. But Yog was neither as discreet or as private as Donny. I guess he took a piss right out in the open. If I know Yog, he was probably pissin' on a statue of the city's founding father and waving at two passing cops for directions at the same time. That sounds like Yog.

Then I guess he took a swing at one of the cops that were

trying to arrest him. That sounds like Yog, too. Have you seen his batting average for this season? Shit, he hasn't hit anything.

Fortunately, the front office was able to keep the story from leaking out until today. Good thing, or George would have really been pissed. But by the time the news leaked out, George had already fined both players one thousand dollars a piece and donated the money to the Save Amateur Sports in New York Foundation, which I thought was a pissin' good idea.

I started, was horseshit, and the Royals finally beat us. Rags got the loss, though, by giving up the winning run in the ninth. He was really pissed.

Monday, May 13 — NEW YORK

We're playin' different under Billy. We're playin' like we're pissed off.

In tonight's game, Whit, who is still pressing, was what is becoming his usual self. He pitched one inning and gave up five runs. He's not exactly what I would call a hard-luck pitcher. In fact, I think "hard to watch" would be much more appropriate.

Then Billy brought in this kid Cooper, who tried but just couldn't better his predecessor. He gave up only three runs in the inning he pitched. So we were down 8–0 after only two innings, but we came back real strong.

Cowls, who didn't even get a chance to leave the other day before he was recalled, completely shut the Twins down for the next seven innings, which gave us a chance to catch up. He just looked like the Cowls of old out there tonight.

Then we finally won it when Donny, who's still pissed off about being arrested the other night, hit a three-run homer in the ninth, to give us a 9–8 win.

Billy Gardner, the Twins' manager, is still really pissed off at Billy for protesting that game in the Metrodump. I don't know what it is about Minnesota, but it just seems to bring the worst out of Billy. I don't know if it's because they were the first team to fire him or what, but he's always in rare form when we're there.

Personally, I just think he likes givin' those guys the red ass. He gets a real big kick out of it. I don't know if it gives us any extra advantage as a team, but it sure makes him laugh.

Tonight, Gardner said that he thought Billy's protest was ridiculous and that he was going to retaliate by protestin' any games here in which he felt that his players were affected by playing under the moon.

"If we miss a ball, we're gonna complain that we lost it in the Big Dipper," he said.

Billy'll make damn moonies of all these guys yet.

Tuesday, May 14 — NEW YORK

This piss-ant story about Yog and Donny is gettin' way outta hand. I just can't believe that the media is still talkin' about it around here. I mean, what man hasn't taken a piss outdoors one time or another, sometime in his life.

I think that Billy is the only guy around here with any authority who sees this situation for what it really is. Maury Allen of the *Post* went into Billy's office the other day to interview him about the incident and Billy was really straight with him. He told Maury that when he was a kid, he and his buddies used to practice writing their names in the dirt while pissing. Then I heard that he offered to demonstrate right then and there, which I bet sent Maury scurryin' out of his office like he was running from a fire.

We came from behind again and won. The key hit was Griff's grand slam in the seventh. He may not be happy here but he's out there givin' it all he's got, which could only help to increase his market value tremendously, which I'm sure makes George smile.

Fish wasn't that great tonight, but he still got the win in relief. He had those suckers backin' out of there all night. And it's hard as hell to get good wood on the ball when your ass is closer to the box seats than to the plate.

Count was the starter tonight but he looked terrible. I think his hip is still botherin' him. Hell, you'd need a calculator just to Count up all the hits he gave up.

Wednesday, May 15 — NEW YORK

To preserve their precious image, Yankees owners have always hired private eyes—leadfoots, gumshoes—to keep an eye on their boys. I guess it all started back with Babe Ruth. And from what I heard, Babe forced many a leadfoot either into early retirement or into insane asylums. Hell, he just never gave the guys a day or a night off and eventually it became hard just to find a guy that would volunteer to trail him. A true Yankee.

The tradition that Babe established has been passed along through the years, from generation to generation of great Yankees players. From DiMagg to Mantle to today.

Billy still loves to tell the story about his and Mickey's personal leadfoot, a guy that had been following them around for months, a guy that they had grown affectionately close to, a guy severely over-worked. One night Billy and Mick came down to the hotel lobby and found their leadfoot, in complete disguise of course, waiting there for them. Over the last few months, though, this gumshoe had followed them almost everywhere they went, but neither Mick nor Billy let on that they knew he was there. They didn't want to hurt the guy's feelings and make him think that he wasn't doin' a good job.

But this one night must have been a special case, 'cause supposedly Mick felt so sorry for the guy, who'd been out followin' them around all night long for the last few evenings, that he felt that the guy deserved a break. So he went up to the gumshoe and told him that he and Billy were just gonna be goin' out to dinner and that he was free to take the next few hours off. Then Mick gave him the name and address of a bar that they were gonna be at later and told him to meet them there.

In another incident, Tony Kubek and another player went out one night for a milkshake and were followed of course by a gumshoe. When they got to where they were goin', Kubek bought a milkshake, not only for his buddy, but also for the leadfoot who'd followed them and now was sittin' across the restaurant from him.

And in doin' his part to preserve this part of our proud tradition,

George has his leadfoots too. They're all around. And as part of our duty to try and uphold our end of such a proud tradition, one that dates all the way back to the great Babe, we do our best to keep these leadfoots busy. Hell, even when I'm dead on my feet and don't feel like goin' out, I still do, just to help preserve the tradition. And when I wake up the next morning with a splitting hangover, I feel good because I know that I have done my best to help preserve this proud aspect of our tradition.

Billy feels the same way. He may take it to extremes at times, but he only does so because of his love for this organization and all that it stands for. He just loves this tradition so much that he's just willing to do anything, even stay out partying all night, every night, if that's what it takes to preserve the image and tradition of this great organization that has been with us for so long. Billy Martin: not a drunk, not a rowdy. No! Billy Martin: a true Yankee, who's willing to sacrifice even his deep-rooted morals for the preservation of a great piece of Americana.

Baylor and a few of the other guys went over to Lou's place in Kansas City Saturday night, and as usual they were followed by a few leadfoots.

When they got to Lou's, Baylor and his bunch were given a table next to another table housing two young ladies. An innocent conversation ensued between the two tables and somewhere in the idle chitchat, one of the players mentioned that he had a headache (now that's a switch for ya). So one of the ladies started rummaging through her purse to see if she had any aspirin and wound up pulling out a bottle of Tylenol, which she handed to the player.

Which sent the leadfoots, sittin' a few tables away, absolutely berserk. I guess one of them was so anxious to see what was goin' on—this must have been his first drug bust—that he tried to hurdle a table or two standing between them and ended up almost castrating himself on another customer's raised fork.

Either way, the story concerning the entire Tylenol incident was leaked to the press this week, and George got really pissed. There's no way that he wants the image of his organization tarnished by the fact that his players accept Tylenol from strangers.

. . .

We finally got to the .500 mark with a 6–5, ten-inning win over Texas tonight. Guid was great but we just couldn't get him any runs. So Rags picked up the win in relief. This come-from-behind Billyball shit is gettin' hard for me to take. If it keeps up, I may be retired by the All Star break.

Thursday, May 16 — NEW YORK

It was Billy's fifty-seventh birthday today. Fifty-seven chronologically, that is. Shit, physically the man must be about 104. Hell, he just never stops. He gets more out of one evening out than some folks do out of an entire lifetime. But that's our Billy, and we love him just as old and as crotchety as he can be.

Though we didn't do it deliberately, I guess you could say that we celebrated his birthday by winning in typical Billy Martin fashion. Again, I remind you, that was totally unintentional. Shit, personally I would have much rather won it the easy way. But that's just not our style.

We started out behind, as usual, but then we battled back to tie 'em. Then the Rangers took the lead again. Then we tied 'em again and eventually won it in the bottom of the ninth, when Hendy scored on Winnie's bases-loaded force out. Typical Billy Martin baseball: excitement and intrigue from wire to wire.

Doug Rader was fired as manager of the Rangers today. I guess this loss was kinda the straw that broke the camel's back. Bobby Valentine was hired to replace him.

I kinda liken the firing of a big league manager to the exposure of a guy's wife foolin' around on him. Shit, everybody knows before the husband, the damn neighbors, their kids, their dogs, their damn cats, the postman, milkman, everybody.

The firin' of Rader, I guess, was no big surprise. But it was done in a dastardly way. Shit, Valentine was already hired, moved in, and running the team before they finally let Rader go. Shit, I might have to give some second thoughts to being a big league manager. I just don't like this shit. In fact, as I see it, there might be a hell of a lot more security in just bein' a fifty-year-old knuckleball pitcher.

Friday, May 17 — CALIFORNIA

George kept Montefusco home from this roadtrip so he could rest and receive treatment, but it sounds like more of a punishment to me. George also ordered our assistant trainer, Mark Letendre, and our strength coach, Jack McDowell, to stay home, so they could take care of Montefusco, who really only needs about forty-five minutes worth of treatment a day.

Though it may sound like a vacation for all three guys, at least for Mark and Jack it isn't. They're supposed to be in here at nine o'clock every morning and aren't allowed to leave until five o'clock in the afternoon, no matter what time Montefusco shows up for his treatment. George just believes in running things like a business around here, whether there's work to be done or not.

Every big leaguer has some team that he especially hits or pitches well against. For me, that team is the Angels. I don't know why, but I've owned them so far this season. I just wish that I could bottle up whatever magic I hold over them and use it against the rest of the league.

Tonight, I gave up only two singles in seven and two-thirds, as Guid—yes Guid—and I and Coops shut out the Angels, 6–0, for my two hundred and eighty-ninth career win.

Saturday, May 18 — CALIFORNIA

My dad is in the hospital again, which is not unusual for him. I called down to Atlanta, who's on the Game of the Week, to see if Joe Garagiola would wish him well over the air. That always brightens my dad up.

My dad's been pretty sick for about the last twelve years. It all started when he hurt himself comin' out of a factory after working late one night. He fell on a sheet of ice and screwed up his shoulder when he tried to use his arm to brace himself for the fall.

He should have gone to the hospital right then and there, to have it fixed, but he never went. In fact, as kids none of us ever went to a doctor or a hospital. We just couldn't afford it. Our cure was usually a bowl of homemade chicken soup or a shot of whiskey mixed with some honey and lemon. We always just kinda let nature take its course.

The shoulder injury eventually stopped my dad from ever working again. It just healed the wrong way and he could no longer straighten it out. The whole situation was very depressing for my father, a man still in the prime of his life, a hardworking man who didn't know the meaning of a day off. To him, not being able to work meant not really having a reason to live. He began seeing himself as more of a burden than anything, and he hated feeling that way. He could no longer fish, hunt, or hang out with his buddies. He was losing his will and reason to live.

Eventually he grew depressed and pneumonia set in and we had to put him in the hospital. Then after he got home, he started having these dizzy spells that scared the shit outta me. Our doctor told us that his spells were being caused by some corroded veins in his neck that led to his brain, which weren't allowing enough oxygen to get to his brain.

Shortly after, he was back in the hospital with pneumonia. While he was there, they discovered that he had a blood clot in his lung. That was in August of '73, when I pitched my no-hitter against San Diego. Right then and there I discovered just how much of an effect my pitching had on my father. I mean, I always knew that he really cared, but this time I felt that my no-hitter was the only thing that kept him alive. I felt that it did much more for him than any doctor, any nurses, or any medicine could possibly do. As I saw it, my pitching became one of my father's main reasons for living. It could never replace all that he had lost the power to do, all that he loved so much, but now it was all that he had to live for, and that experience in '73 showed me that.

But my father didn't get any better. In fact, he's gotten steadily worse. When he got home from the hospital, he began having circulation problems with his legs, the arm ached more, the dizziness got worse. He became a prisoner in his own home.

Finally, I talked him into going to the Cleveland Clinic, where a doctor said he thought he could help him. When we got there, he was put in a room with a guy from Atlanta who was experiencing the same dizziness problems as my father. The man from Atlanta decided to try the surgery, which some of the other doctors called risky, but he lived and is much improved today.

My mother wouldn't let my father go through with the surgery. She was just so scared of losing him. And now he's gone downhill so far that he wouldn't be able to go through with it if he had to. It just kills me to see him like this, but now more than ever I realize how important my pitching is to him. To see Joe's and my name in a box score in a newspaper every five days or hear our name occasionally on a televised game is all that my father lives for.

Since Monty went back on the Disabled List, Cowls has gotten another chance to start, and he's doin' much better. He picked up his second consecutive win tonight. Fish pitched the last two and two-thirds and got his first save, as we beat the Angels, 6–1.

Sunday, May 19 — CALIFORNIA

I think we've finally found a cure for what's been ailin' Whit. Bo Derek was sittin' in the seats behind the plate today and she was lookin' real great, tight sweater and all.

Whit just couldn't take his eyes off of her. So we told him just to focus on ol' Bo and let the ball go. His control improved 100 percent. Unfortunately, later in the game he got a blister on his index finger from exerting too much pressure on the ball and had to leave the game. But even though he lost this one, he didn't deserve to. But at least we may have finally found a cure for what's been ailin' Whit. Now all we have to do is find a Bo Derek look-alike to attend all our games.

Monday, May 20, OFF DAY — BELLAIRE, OHIO

Dad didn't sound like he was doin' real good so, since today was an off-day, I decided to fly home and visit him.

Over the years, trips like this have become kinda routine for me, even more for Joe, who caters to my dad's needs much more than I do. I guess it's just a difference in how we approach things. Joe's always flyin' home to be with him. He'll sit there in my dad's hospital room rubbin' his back, holdin' his hands, and waitin' on him hand and foot.

Me, I don't make as many trips home to see my dad 'cause I don't want to scare him. Hell, I know that I'd be scared shitless if every time I got sick my boys flew in from wherever to be with me.

No, where Joe takes to comforting my dad, I challenge him, just like he used to do to us as kids. He always told us that if there was somethin' that you wanted you had to go out and get it. And I know that he wants to see Joe win No. 200, me No. 300, and for both of us to someday play on the same team and to appear in a World Series. Where Joe comforts him, I just challenge him to stay around long enough to see all of this happen. I just never let him forget what he taught us: that if you want something, you gotta go out and get it. And right now, I don't think there's anything that he wants more than to see Joe and me accomplish all that we've set out to do.

Tuesday, May 21—SEATTLE

People may make fun of Billy and all the complainin' he does. But in his own weird way, he does get his point across. Look at what happened with the Metrodump. He bitched like hell about that place and today it was announced in the paper that the Twins were gonna spend approximately $100,000 to get the lighting fixed.

I think Billy'd make a great lobbyist for just about anything. I can just see him runnin' up and kickin' dirt on the president or a congressman or somethin'. He'd get his point across one way or another. That's just Billy. If he can pass that shit he does past these umps, he can get it past anyone.

The West Coast has been kind of a disaster area for Eastern clubs over the years. Just too many tan fannies and time changes. But we seem to be doin' pretty well this time around.

Guid won again tonight. He pitched eight strong innings and Coop finished up.

I think too many people are givin' Billy too much credit, though, for Guid's revitalization. I think the credit should go Guid's way. It was Guid, himself, who decided to make the change in his pitching style, and he decided to do so way before Billy ever re-re-re-re-rejoined the team. It just so happened that he finally got the hang of it after Billy got here. But Billy's not the one that deserves the credit. That should go to Guid.

Wednesday, May 22 — SEATTLE

The Mariners have got this kid by the name of Young. He's 15–27 against the rest of the league and 4–1 lifetime against us. Some players just hate some teams for whatever reason. I think that might be the case here.

Well, tonight the kid stuck our bats up our asses again. Too bad too, 'cause Rassy went the whole way and pitched a hell of a game. But Young just got the better of him tonight.

Rumor has it that the Yanks have been tryin' to get Ken Phelps from the Mariners. Phelps' resemblance to Reggie Jackson is amazing. Phelps swings from the left side, has a lot of pop in his bat, attended Arizona State, and wears No. 44.

Billy has always taken a lot of unfair criticism from the media over the years (or at least that's what he believes), which has really tainted his image, even in the eyes of his own family. The other day Billy said that someone asked his granddaughter what he did for a livin' and she replied, "He kicks dirt on umpires."

Thursday, May 23 — SEATTLE

We took an early lead tonight, but Phelps took me deep for his first grand slam and we wound up losin' 6–4.

As if I didn't feel bad enough, Don Baylor, our team captain, came over to my locker after the game and told me that I had been fined $500 for givin' up the granny, like I had intentionally done so or somethin'. Right away I stood up and looked him right in the eye, 'cause I was pissed as hell. But I could see how embarrassed he was, so I calmed right down.

But being fined around here is almost common procedure. It's supposed to fulfill two purposes. One, it's supposed to make George feel better. And, two, it's supposed to be a way that Billy can keep George off his ass. But, shit, George orders Billy to give out fines as freely as some folks give out candy on Halloween.

I guess that it used to be common procedure for George to come down into the clubhouse and make rah-rah speeches for the guys, which either used to drive the guys crazy or into hysterics.

Well, when George asked Billy to come back, I heard that as part of their agreement, George promised not to give any more of his goddamn talks; and Billy promised to employ more discipline, which meant that he'd fine more guys. So instead of comin' down to reprimand us personally, George now just calls down to the dugout and has Billy fine us, which is not normally Billy's style, but it does keep George off his ass.

Then Billy passes the buck to Baylor, whose job it is to collect the fines. But in all honesty, Billy doesn't give a shit one way or the other whether Don collects the money or not. All Billy wants is to get George off his ass. Then if George asks him, Billy can honestly say that he fined whomever.

But even though all this shit may keep Billy's ass safe and secure, it's unconstitutional and a real pain in the ass for us. I mean, it's bad enough when I get fined for givin' up a granny, but it's even worse when George calls down to the dugout during a game and has Mark Connors, our pitching coach, fine Rich Bordi $100 for not havin' his mustache trimmed.

About the worst thing I ever saw a guy fined for, though, was when Bobby Meacham was fined for swinging at a first pitch. It happened in the eighth or ninth inning of a game, we were down by a run and with a man in scoring position. In that situation, it's Meach's job to get the run across, no matter how he does it. He just happened to choose the first pitch to swing at. Unfortunately, he popped it up and it cost him $250.

It's just not justice or the American way. Anybody could take George to court for the simple principle of the thing—and you'd win easily. But you'd lose in the long run. 'Cause you'd find your ass in Columbus or some fuckin' place like that the very next day.

Saturday, May 25 — OAKLAND

What had started out as a pretty good roadtrip for us is beginning to look dismal. For the third night in a row, we lost to a team we probably should have beat.

Whit started, but Bo didn't show, so he reverted back to his old self. He lasted only five innings and gave up three runs. But he didn't get the loss. That went to Rags, who walked in the winning run with two out in the ninth. Which sent Billy flyin' out of the dugout screamin' at the top of his lungs, callin' Dave Kingman a "rockhead," 'cause he said the big guy stepped out of the baseline.

Hey, Billy'll do anything to win a game. Including risk his life by insulting the biggest, strongest man in the game today.

Sunday, May 26 — OAKLAND

Don Mattingly was out for the second game in a row with a pulled groin muscle but we still managed to score a 13–1 win, surprisingly our highest run total of the year. Guid, who's become our stopper once again, was the benefactor as he improved his record to 5–3.

Today marked a very significant day in Yankee history—Bob Shirley, our comical reliever, got into a damn game. According to Billy, plans for his use of Shirls in today's game actually started nine months ago, when Rich Bordi's wife got pregnant. Because if Bordi had been here instead of with his wife, who was delivering, Shirls would have never got in.

Monday, May 27 — OAKLAND

Rags, who has had a tough time comin' back from a fractured toe, got beat again. Dwayne Murphy took him deep in the bottom of the ninth to win it for the A's. Too bad, 'cause Rassy, who went eight and two-thirds, pitched real good again.

. . .

Once upon a time Omar Moreno was a great outfielder. Then he signed a huge contract with Houston, got traded to us and then got lost in the damn shuffle. Right now, he's just a $700,000-a-year pinch-runner/defensive replacement.

Omar doesn't normally say anything, even though I'm sure he's plenty pissed about not playin'. But today, he stormed into Billy's office and demanded to know why he wasn't playin'.

Billy, who didn't even flinch or even look up from what he was reading, replied, "Rickey Henderson, Dave Winfield, Ken Griffey." The question around here is if Omar will ever be heard from again.

Wednesday, May 29 — NEW YORK

My knuckler was really workin' today, but then when isn't it against the Angels? I pitched eight scoreless innings and gave up only two hits, then Rich Bordi came in to finish up for me. It was the two-hundred-ninetieth win of my career.

This strike shit is really beginnin' to heat up around here, and I was hopin' that we'd ended that shit once and for all in '83.

Already the owners are startin' to work the public for sympathy and the union is tryin' to force solidarity among its members. The battle lines are bein' drawn. Today, the owners and twenty-six player reps got together in New York for something like the thirtieth time this year. The owners squawked about goin' broke and the player reps moaned about the protection of the free enterprise system.

Today was also our day to take the ceremonial strike vote, the players' rebuttal to the owners' pleas, which is somewhat ridiculous, as far as I'm concerned. 'Cause nobody really knows what the hell the issues really are. Most of us just sit there dumbfounded as one of the guys from the union "objectively" goes over the things that need to be considered.

Then after he goes over all 250 things that need to be considered in his rapid twenty-minute presentation, we're asked to narrow our choice down to a simple yes or no vote.

We voted 25–0 to strike. But if all the issues had been weighed and considered individually, I don't think the response for a strike would have been nearly as positive as it turned out.

Ted just returned from a trip to the Soviet Union and it looks like Eddie Hass, whose club has been faltering terribly, is on his way to Siberia. Right now, it looks as if Yog has the inside track to get the job. But he hasn't been able to be reached for comment 'cause he's continually out on the golf course taking advantage of that paid vacation that came along with him being fired last April.

Thursday, May 30 — NEW YORK

Reggie stirred up so much shit around here that anytime he returns home to play the Yanks it's a real big event. But he's been kinda disappointing for the fans in this series. Last night, he ended the game by pinch-hitting into a double play. Tonight, he did absolutely nothin' and ended the game by striking out.

I guess it's just hard for anyone that lived through the Reggie era to come to grips with the fact that he's no longer here. In fact, I bet that George was so pissed off about Reg's poor showin' that he may have even tried to fine him. Guys like Reggie are just hard to forget.

Cowls seems to be gettin' that ol' confidence back again. He went seven and two-thirds and gave up only three hits and a run. Rags, who appears to be back on the track now also, finished up for him and struck out four of the five batters he faced.

But the big news of the night was that a star was born, or so they say. His name is Dan Pasqua, a young, left-handed-hitting power hitter, who hit his first big league homer tonight. They're already calling him the next Mickey Mantle, which might do more harm for the kid than good.

What he really needs, more than anything else at this time, is to concentrate on his hitting. He shouldn't even be bothered with creating an image or with livin' up to someone else's expectations of him. Clubs are always guilty of doin' that to their young players. It seems like they're always lookin' for legends.

Well, this kid may be it, 'cause he can really swing the bat. But

I just hope that they don't ruin him like they've done with so many other potential Mantles and DiMaggios in the past.

During the fourth inning of tonight's game, Henry Cotto, one of our reserve outfielders, asked Gene Monahan, our head trainer, for a cotton swab so that he could clean out his ears.

Gene gave him the swab and Henry walked over to the bat rack and started cleaning out his ears. Griff came over and reached up for his batting helmet, accidentally hitting Cotto's hand and driving the cotton swab well into his ear and breaking his eardrum. Cotto had to be rushed to the hospital.

Billy just went wild and jumped all over Gene's ass like it was all his fault for giving Henry the swab in the first place.

"You've been in baseball for over twenty fuckin' years," he screamed at Monahan. "How could you let something like that happen? That was the most fuckin' incompetent thing I ever fuckin' saw!" I'm sure we're only a few days away from having cotton swabs banned from both the dugout and clubhouse. That'd be like banning toilet paper.

Friday, May 31—NEW YORK

I just can't imagine anyone firing as many managers as George. But according to today's newspaper, Charlie Finley, the former owner of the Oakland A's, fired fifteen managers in his stint in the big leagues. George, up to this point (and not including what may happen later this week), has fired only twelve.

I wonder if George knows about this shit. 'Cause I know that he just hates finishing second to anyone in anything. I wonder how they rank on firing PR guys and secretaries. I'll have to ask Safety.

Whit was his usual self tonight, and Billy alerted the bullpen to be ready even before the playin' of the national anthem. Whit, who's still pushing too hard, gave up three runs in the first two innings and was gone by the end of the fourth.

Fish came in and pitched the last five innings and didn't even allow a run. He got the win, which marked our tenth straight victory under Billy at home. This damn place was just made for him.

Saturday, June 1—NEW YORK

The club announced today that on June 14, a bunch of Disneyland characters were gonna perform before our game with the Tigers. Can you just imagine that? Mickey, Goofy, and the Bronx Zoo—all in one night! It'll be too much for almost anyone to handle; that is, with the exception of Billy. He's real used to the craziness around here. In fact, I think he kinda likes it.

Guid got his fifth straight win tonight by going all the way and allowing only two runs. If we're gonna get back into this thing, he's gonna be the one to lead us there.

Sunday, June 2—NEW YORK

Billy was in rare form today. I don't know if it was because George made him have his picture taken with Mickey and Goofy or what, but he was totally out of control. Some guys just don't like ol' Mick and the big Goof.

But by game time, he had lost it. We were all just kinda sittin' around waitin' for him to erupt or a reason for him to erupt. Then this kid Cooper, who he brought into the game to replace Rassy, threw Domingo Ramos a fastball on the first pitch, which is like a cardinal sin around here, and Ramos deposited it in the left-field bleachers, and that was enough of a reason for Billy. He went berserk. At the end of the inning, he ran out halfway to home plate to meet Hass and started the confrontation right there. Then after he was done with Hass, he ran over and gave Cooper an earful. By the time he was finished with the both of 'em, they were feelin' lower than low.

Supposedly this all started because Billy doesn't allow any of his pitchers to throw a fastball to any Latins on the first pitch. But I think he just had the red ass because of havin' to be photographed with the Mick and Goofy.

Then a little later in the game, Rich Bordi threw a fastball to Al Cowens, an Afro-American, on the first pitch, and Cowens hit it out. Billy went berserk again. Shit, and Cowens isn't even Latin. Hass ended up gettin' another earful, and Billy just mothered Bordi into total embarrassment.

Then, if that wasn't bad enough, an inning later the Mariners had a guy on first, and Hass kept lookin' over to Billy for the keep-'em-close sign to give to Bordi, but Billy never gave it. So Hass just let Rich come to the plate and the guy wound up stealin' the base. It took ten of us to keep Billy from runnin' out onto the field and rippin' Hass's head off.

But that's just the way things are around here. Sometimes you're wrong even when you're right. About the only guys that get a kick out of Billy when he's like this are our opponents. Just the other night, when we were playin' California, Juan Beniquez came walkin' to the plate, whistled at Hass, and held up his index finger, just like Billy does every time a Latin player comes to the plate, to remind whoever's catchin' about this first-ball, fastball shit. We all about died laughin', and Billy just kinda looked at us real strange, like we were the ones who were screwed up. He's a real serious son of a gun on the bench. About the only time he'd laugh while in the dugout is if Earl Weaver, Gene Mauch, Mickey, or Goofy got hit in the nuts with a foul tip or somethin'. Otherwise, he's all business.

Chuck Cottier's team has been strugglin' this year, and today, Chuck, usually a mild-mannered type of guy, just lost it. After protestin' a check swing and bein' ejected, he ran out to first base, next to the accusin' ump, uprooted first base, and grabbed everything within reach—helmets, bats, balls, bat boys, ushers—and threw it all into right field. It was one of the greatest exhibitions of total frustration and outright madness I'd ever seen.

What was ol' laid-back Billy's opinion of Cottier's tirade? "He's gotta learn to control himself," said the maddest of the game's madmen.

I guess the cussin' out Hass and Bordi were given wasn't enough of a punishment, 'cause they were fined too. But it kinda worries me that Coop wasn't fined. I wonder what they have in mind for him?

Monday, June 3 — NEW YORK

Coops was sent down to Columbus today. I guess he should just feel lucky that he's still in this country. I could just see Billy sendin' him down to the jungles of Panama to learn how to pitch to head-hunters. Mike Armstrong was recalled to take his place.

I wasn't as excited about gettin' win No. 291 tonight as I was intent on avoiding any confrontation with Billy. I even took to hidin' my Mickey Mouse watch and my Mickey Mouse Club ears before I took the mound tonight. I can just see him findin' that stuff in my locker. He'd go berserk and send me up to the plate to hit, which is a rarity for a pitcher in this damn league, and order the opposing pitcher to take his best shot, a first-ball fastball aimed right for the love nest.

He just doesn't like ol' Mick and Goofy. Maybe he never had a childhood and seein' any of those guys like Bugs, Don Duck, or Mick and Goofy just reminds him of that fact? Right from the crib to reform school.

Tuesday, June 4 — NEW YORK

Billy's got a shit list for guys that screw up, and he keeps 'em on it until he feels like forgivin' 'em. Bordi was placed on it yesterday. But with the way our pitchin' is goin' and considerin' how well Rich has been pitchin', it won't be too long before Billy will have to let him off it and get him back into the normal scheme of things.

Bob Shirley is the resident incumbent on Billy's shit list. Shirls has been on it since Billy was last here but nobody, not Shirls or even Billy, seems to remember why. So Shirls just sits out there in the bullpen takin' up space.

Hell, now he doesn't even pitch enough to get a chance to screw up, unless you count battin' practice. Maybe he's in the shit-house 'cause he pitches lousy BP or somethin'. No one seems to know. But it doesn't seem to be anything personal between the two. They get along fine. I just think that Billy feels that Shirls is a horseshit pitcher.

• • •

I held Kingman pretty well intact last night, which Billy really loved, 'cause he hates old Kong, for whatever reason. Even with all the dingers the big guy hits, he'd be in Billy's shithouse if he had him, just for the general principle of the thing, of course.

I struck out Kong three straight times last night before Rags came in in the ninth and gave up a homer to him. But Kong took Cowls deep early tonight and gave the A's all the runs they needed as they beat us, 2–0.

Wednesday, June 5 — NEW YORK

We start a twenty-six game stretch against Eastern Division foes in Milwaukee tomorrow. With the way we've been playin' and as far out as we are, it looks like it'll be a critical stretch for us. If we want to get back in this thing, we got to do it now.

George cancelled tonight's game early this afternoon, which really pissed off the A's. They started callin' it the Ed Whitson Rainout, 'cause it's no secret that we're hurtin' for starting pitching and if we had our druthers we'd rather have Whit start tomorrow against the Brewers instead of tonight against the A's.

But then the A's really started to cause a stink when the rain stopped only a short while after George cancelled the game. They started complainin' that George cancelled the game simply because they were a lousy draw, which they truly are, and because he wanted Whit to pitch tomorrow instead of tonight. Now, would George do that?

Thursday, June 6 — MILWAUKEE

I've been gettin' pretty tired of all these reporters chasing me around askin' me if I would be interested in takin' over as the Braves' manager if Ted fired Eddie Haas, who hasn't been doin' too good. For weeks I've been dodgin' their questions with "no comments," "I don't knows," or "I don't want to talk about its."

But they know I'm bullshitting 'em, so they just keep comin' back each day, and I've been gettin' real tired of it. So today, I said to myself, "Screw it, I'm gonna tell 'em exactly what they want to hear."

So when the first reporter came up to me and routinely asked me about goin' back to Atlanta, expecting to hear my routine answer, I knocked his socks off by just sayin', "Yes."

That's all these guys needed to hear. One word and I was front-page news, the talk of the day.

Whit got the shit kicked out of him today. I think that he had just one too many days rest. He lasted only four and two-thirds and gave up nine hits, one of his better outings. What a shame to waste it and what a way to start an important stretch like this, with a loss to the Brewers.

Mom called again today. She still hasn't gotten her caps from George. All the time she was talkin' to me I could hear her pounding her umbrella against the leg of her chair. Very sternly, she asked me if she should drive up and see George about all this. I said, "Sure, I've always heard that George has a special yearning to be a soprano."

Friday, June 7— MILWAUKEE

It's amazing how fast news travels. By the time the news of my story hit the streets this morning, I'd already had several people call me about working for me in Atlanta, and about three-fourths of the team came over and talked to me about movin' down there with me. There were infielders, pitchers, outfielders, catchers, many of whom were starters, plus trainers, PR men, clubhouse guys, ushers, secretaries, and even reporters. Shit, enough guys contacted me that I could start my own team—and have a damn good one too. It's be like transferring the whole organization, hangers-on and all, down to Atlanta.

Almost everybody wants out of here—except Billy, of course. I guess that just goes to show ya how nuts he is.

Guid, Rags, everybody but Winnie, Baylor and Hendy, were horseshit tonight as we lost to the Brewers again, this time in the tenth inning.

Saturday, June 8 — MILWAUKEE

We finally beat Milwaukee, but we had to go to the thirteenth inning to do it. Rassy was great tonight, giving up only one run through nine, but we just couldn't drive any runs across for him.

Yog, with his first hit since his dad was axed, finally drove in Winnie in the thirteenth with the winning run.

Sunday, June 9 — MILWAUKEE

I get a lot of respect around here because of my age, but, then, maybe too much respect. I'm the only guy on the club who never has to open a door for himself. And, hell, the other day two boy scouts had the choice of escortin' either an elderly old lady or me across a busy intersection. They chose me.

Billy kinda treats me like that, too. He's always worryin' about me dyin' on the mound or somethin' and he always talks to me like he's talkin' to his grandfather, real loud like I can't hear anymore or somethin'.

He's just got to realize that not everyone is as old at forty-six as he was. In fact, nobody will ever be as old at forty-six as Billy was.

But he's just gotta realize that no one was as well-worn as he was at forty-six. Shit, but he doesn't seem to understand that. He gives me seven days and sometimes eight or nine days rest between starts. Hell, God didn't need that much rest when he was creating the entire world.

I keep tryin' to tell him that I like to pitch every fourth day, but he just keeps lookin' at me and shakin' his head gently, sayin', "O.K. Phil, we'll see what we can do," like I was senile or somethin'. But the honest-to-God truth is that when I get that much rest I'm too strong out on the mound. I know, maybe I should cut back on the spinach, but I'm not kiddin'.

When I go out there after seven days' rest the knuckler moves around all over the place, like a whore on nickel night. I just can't control the son of a bitch, and I end up gettin' behind on a lot of guys. That forces me to come in with my hummer, which could make even a blind batter look like Babe Ruth.

Tonight was one of those cases, and I kinda felt like the center bumper in a pinball game. Balls were flyin' by me left and right. But what was even worse is that Pete Vuckovich, who Phil Rizzuto appropriately said looked like a large pile of soiled clothes, was almost unhittable for seven innings.

I guess that maybe you are gettin' old when a big pile of shitty clothes not only pitches better than you, but looks better, too.

Monday, June 10 — NEW YORK

I guess if there was a crucial game for us this early in the season, tonight's game was it. In such a game, you always make sure that you got your big guy on the mound, your Tom Seaver, Dwight Gooden, Steve Carlton, Nolan Ryan.

For us tonight it was, of course—Bob Shirley. That's right, Bob Shirley, the lowest of Billy's lows, the only guy ever fined for just makin' the team, the man who has to go home to his wife and kids each night and face the embarrassin' question, "Daddy, are you ever gonna pitch again?"

Well, tonight, Shirls got his chance, but not until after Billy had considered all the alternatives. Rags couldn't start because Billy thought it would wind him up too much to bring him out of the bullpen, then send him back again. Fish and Bordi couldn't start 'cause they were just too valuable as relievers. Dom had a date for the night and couldn't make it, and Billy didn't get any takers when he asked for volunteers from the infielders, outfielders, catchers, trainers, and clubhouse guys. So Shirls got his chance.

But he surprised everybody, including the Blue Jays, who probably went out partying real late last night after they heard Billy had picked Shirls to start. Billy was talkin' about wearin' blinders to the damn game; and the infielders supposedly considered orderin' special bullet-proof vests for tonight.

Shirls went six and one-third, gave up only one run and got the win. He attributed his success to the fact that it'd been so long since he pitched the batters actually forgot what he threw; and those that remembered were already retired.

Tuesday, June 11—NEW YORK

It's amazin' what a guy like Shirls can do for a ball club. Tonight, the crowd was *ssssoooo* pumped up from last night's miracle that they were chanting in unison Ed-die, Ed-die-*EEEdddd-ddddiiieee* for Whit, all night long. I guess they wanted another miracle, and he gave 'em one, too.

Whit was great for nine and one-third tonight, givin' up only one run. But we ended up losin' it in the eleventh when Willie Randolph booted a ground ball that eventually led to a 4–1 Toronto win.

I heard that George got so pissed off that he tried to trade Willie right after the game last night to the Padres for Alan Wiggins, who's presently on suspension for drug use.

But all wasn't bad for George today, 'cause the Mets lost to the Phils by a score of 26–7. I'm sure that the only disappointin' aspect of that game for George was that it wasn't on national TV.

Wednesday, June 12 — NEW YORK

Toronto did it to us again, and in extra innings, no less. Right now, they're playin' like a championship club. But I don't know where they got the experience to do so, unless these guys double as hockey players in the off-season.

I just hope that the Mets lost, or Boston, Cleveland—anyone on George's shit list. Otherwise there's gonna be hell to pay around here.

Don Baylor was one of the unhappiest guys when Billy was re-re-re-re-rehired. For some reason the two of them just don't get along, and Don is always quick to let ya know so.

Today, a reporter came up to him and asked him to compare playin' for Yogi to playin' for Billy. Don thought for a minute, then said, "Playin' for Yogi is like playin' for your father. Playin' for Billy is like playin' for your father-in-law."

Thursday, June 13 — NEW YORK

Billy used an opportunity at our off-day workout today (which George had called and Billy was totally against) to blast Clyde King in front of the media, in retaliation for Clyde's comment that Billy should have been usin' Shirls a lot earlier this season.

Well, Billy really let him have it. In fact, he blamed the team's poor fundamental play not on his old buddy Yog, but on Clyde, whose responsibility he said it was to see that the team left spring training ready to play. It was like a beehive around here today. The place was just buzzin' with reporters.

And add to their feud the fact that none of us wanted to be here, were pissed off that we were, as appropriately stated by Don Mattingly, who has a lotta balls for his age, and you'll understand why Graig Nettles once said about this place: "Some kids dream of joining the circus, others of becoming a major league baseball player. As a member of the New York Yankees, I have gotten to do both."

Friday, June 14 — NEW YORK

Billy may be the greatest salesman this world has ever known. Shoot, he could sell a boatload of American flags to the Russians. Today, he sold George on the fact that he didn't say anything to discredit Clyde yesterday and that the dozen or so reporters that had quoted him were all wrong in their assessments. Unbelievable. Billy is just unbelievable.

The next time I go to negotiate a contract, I'm gonna ask Billy to do it for me. By the time he's finished with 'em, he'll have 'em convinced that I'm a tall, slender, blond, blue-eyed twenty-year-old with a blazing knuckleball.

George went for Billy's story, hook, line, and sinker, too, blaming it all on the media. Then in defense of Billy and as kind of a slam against Clyde, George issued a statement sayin' that the only persons permitted to be quoted within the organization were Billy and the players. Notice, no mention of Clyde, the club's GM. I guess birds of a feather really do flock together.

• • •

Detroit came in here and shut us down, 4–0. During a time when we were supposed to be pickin' up ground and movin' back into the pennant race, we're doin' a real shitty job. At the present time, we're in fifth place, eight and a half behind Toronto and only one game ahead of Milwaukee, who's in sixth.

Walt Terrell, the former Met, was the main man today. He and Willie Hernandez combined on the five hitter. The win was Terrell's seventh of the year. A year ago, just about any team could have gotten him from the Mets for a warm body, that is with the exception of us, of course. It would have taken at least half our infield and all our outfield to get him over here. No way they're gonna trade a warm body to us. They just don't happen to care for ol' George.

Saturday, June 15 — NEW YORK

Billy is really playin' this shit to the hilt. Today, he showed up at the park with a tape recorder. He says that he's gonna start recordin' all his interviews. "That way," he said, "I can sue if I'm not quoted accurately."

Then he went on to brag, "Maybe I'll sell them to a newspaper one day for a million dollars." More like Penthouse or Hustler.

But the guy I really feel sorry for is Joe Safety, our PR guy who George has assigned to follow Billy everywhere he goes, to make sure that he isn't harassed by the media. No man has ever been created to be able to fulfill such a task. I don't care if Safety is twenty-five years his junior. Billy has put even more of George's leadfoots in loony bins.

Today was the long awaited Disneyland Day at the stadium, and the biggest clown of all there was not Mickey or Goofy, or even George or Billy, but me. I was totally horseshit, and on national TV, no less. The Tigers just jumped all over my ass, for seven hits and eight runs in two and a third heoric innings.

But I gave the crowd and the TV audience a little bit of everything. I gave 'em walks, runs, home runs, even a balk—Billy told me after the game that George said I had to come in three hours early tomorrow to watch the footage. Now, that's horseshit!

What the hell am I gonna learn from watchin' myself balk over three thousand times. About all I'm gonna learn is how to do it again. George makes it sound like the balk was the low part of my day, the reason that the Tigers jumped all over my ass. Shit, how about the four-run first? Have me come in and watch that for three hours if you really want me to feel bad. But a balk is a balk is a balk, which is boring.

But the minute after Billy told me to come in and review the footage I promptly forgot about it. Heck, no, I'm not comin' in! I wouldn't even get up that early to watch Bugs Bunny, and I'd like watchin' him a whole hell of a lot better than me.

This environment around here isn't for everybody, no matter how much they pay ya. Ask Butch Wynegar, who asked to be traded today. He wants out. I guess part of the reason is because George and Butch reached an agreement, then George pulled the offer off the table.

Sunday, June 16 — NEW YORK

Today was another one of those supposedly crucial games. It seems like we have one of these suckers come up about every ten days around here. Either we're fightin' for a pennant or to help a manager hold onto his job for another week. Who says playin' for the New York Yankees isn't excitin'?

But the reason for the cruciality of today's contest was based around our shortcomings of late, our two straight losses to the Tigers, and our four straight losses total. I guess what we were supposedly fightin' for was just to keep George quiet, which is a major motivating factor around here.

So when we look out to the bullpen to see who's warmin' up for this crucial game, who do we see, but former bullpen hostage, Johnny-on-the-spot, Bob Shirley, master of the seventy-two mile per hour floating fastball, king of Billy's shithouse.

But Shirls, talent or no talent—and that point is severely debatable—came on and did it again for us. Today, he held the red-hot Tigers to four hits and one run over nine. Amazin'!

. . .

Billy was in rare form today, as is normal for any manager in a losing streak; ask Chuck Cottier. He was all over the home-plate ump Tim McClelland's ass today. But McClelland handled it pretty well. Hell, these umps must train in a nut house, which is still nothin' compared to what it is like around here.

But finally in the middle innings, McClelland had enough, or was just tryin' to save a little face, and came over to the dugout and gave us a choice of who we wanted thrown out. Billy pointed right to Guid. So McClelland ran him out of the game. And like a good little big leaguer, Guid took his medicine well, walking quietly up the runway to the clubhouse, showering, then drivin' home. Now that's sacrificin' for the team.

I was lucky because no one noticed that I didn't come in early today. But then I would have rather been fined than have to watch three hours of footage on myself anyway. But I wasn't, 'cause this is just one of those rules that Billy doesn't agree with George on anyway.

In a major move today, Willie Horton, our designated tranquility coach (we're the only team in baseball with one of these—whatever the hell they are) was moved from the bench, where he was demonstratin' for all of us how to be tranquil, to first base, and Mark Connor, our pitchin' coach, was moved out to the bullpen to answer Billy's phone calls. Now if this doesn't bring us a pennant, I don't know what will.

Monday, June 17 — BALTIMORE

Guid, fresh from a night off, looked great as he shut out the Orioles 10–0, giving the Great Earl of Weaver his first loss this year and bringin' a real big smile to ol' Billy's face. Beatin' Weaver brings about as much joy to his heart as the Mets gettin' beat 30–0 on national TV would bring to George's.

Besides, Guid, Hendy, Mattingly and Winnie were the big stars tonight. Between them, they had ten hits in thirteen at-bats, drove in six runs and scored four more.

Billy has taken to batting Mattingly second against left-handers, which may seem rather odd, to move the best third-place hitter in the league up a notch, but it really works, as it did tonight. If nothin' else, it scares the shit out of the opposition. Can you just imagine havin' to face Hendy, Mattingly and Winnie in succession, three to four times a game?

Butch has been talkin' about gettin' outta here, and tonight he got his wish, though probably not in the way he had planned it. He was kneelin' in the on-deck circle when a foul ball flew off the bat of Willie Randolph and hit him right smack in the head. Thank God for batting helmets.

Butch went right down, just like if he had been shot with a gun. The environment around here must be really gettin' to Butch, 'cause rumor has it that instead of seein' stars he began seein' little starry faces of Billy floating around his head, then he collapsed into shock. I guess the Bronx Zoo just isn't for everybody.

Tuesday, June 18 — BALTIMORE

Last week a bullpen hostage, this week the American League's Player of the Week—that's our Bob Shirley. Somebody at the league office must be havin' a real laugh over this one. I know we are. I bet even Shirls is chucklin' to himself about all this.

The guys just couldn't believe it when the news was announced today. In the hotel lobby, everybody just kinda walked by him in awe, afraid to talk to him or anything, like he was some kind of God or somethin'.

Some of the guys scrambled up to him today and asked him for his autograph, which the still somewhat modest Shirls gave without even battin' an eye, like it was an everyday occurrence. Billy just walked by him with a real shitty little grin on his face and said, "*Aawwwww*, shit," and then started to chuckle to himself, like he'd just pulled the wool over somebody's eyes again. When he got to the ballpark, Baylor fined him for impersonating a pitcher. Some guys just get no respect!

Cowls, who hadn't started in twelve days, held the Orioles pretty well intact for five innings before his back stiffened and Billy brought in Rags. Which is kinda early for Rags, but Billy really wanted to win this one badly, what with enjoying beating Earl as much as he does and all.

Fish finished up by pitching the ninth and got the save. Hendy was again one of our big stars. He went five for five last night and three for four tonight and scored three runs. George could double his $1.7 million-a-year salary and he'd still be worth every penny, considering all that he does for this team.

It looks like Butch'll be O.K. He's made it through the most difficult part of his recovery. The visions of Billy have disappeared and the stars have returned.

Wednesday, June 19 — BALTIMORE

Winnie went four for five tonight and drove in three runs. Mike Pagliarulo, our young third baseman, went three for five. Hendy went two for four, and Whit pitched his first shutout of the year.

But Ron Hassey, if you can believe it, was the big star. Hey, anytime Hass gets two hits in a game, let alone two dingers, he should be the hero. Shit, he's only done that about once in his career and that was back in T-ball when his team was playin' a team full of blind kids.

With all the bench jockeys and bullpen hostages, and even Whit, coming to the forefront this week, the whole scenario kinda reminds me of the movie *Revenge of the Nerds*. But that's the true beauty of this club. When all seems hopeless, another overpaid, talented, yet forgotten, hero surfaces to save your butt.

We're now only five and a half games out of the top spot, which Toronto presently occupies, and which really has Billy laughin' and smilin', cause he finally has some justification for goin' out and doin' all this celebratin'. Though I'm not sure which motivation is stronger, the fact that we're back in the pennant race or the fact that we just beat ol' Earl three straight. I'm puttin' my money on the beating of Earl.

A story came out of Atlanta today which said that the Braves were interested in landing both Joe and me after the season, since we would both be free agents. I must admit that both Joe and I have already given a considerable amount of thought to the subject. In fact, our sister, Phyllis, has already come up with a slogan we could use: "Phil and Joe and away we go."

My mom was interviewed for the piece. She likes that kinda stuff. But I'm glad that she didn't use the opportunity to cuss out ol' George about not sending her her hats. The kinda things she is planning to say to him should be said behind closed doors, not through the newspapers. But then I don't know if they could print it anyway.

Thursday, June 20 — DETROIT

What has happened to Mike Armstrong here is the perfect example of what I was afraid would happen to me. He's a good young pitcher who had some pretty good years in Kansas City as Quisenberry's set-up guy.

In '82, he was 5–5, with a 3.20 ERA. Then the next year, he went 10–7, with a 3.86 ERA. Then George, needing a set-up guy for Rags, got him for Steve Balboni and Roger Erickson.

Whoever the manager was at that time had big plans for Army and thought that he'd fit right in in front of Rags, the way Ron Davis used to fit in so nicely in front of Goose. But somehow, as often happens—ask Shirls—he got lost in the shuffle and found himself in the shithouse. And now he's really frustrated and confused. He doesn't know what the fuck he did wrong, when actually the truth is that he hasn't done anything wrong. He just got screwed.

But as a player, that's hard to accept. You always seem to blame yourself. You start feelin' like you gave them a reason to do this to you. You start feelin' that you're not earning your money. You start seein' every opportunity that you get to pitch as a crucial point in your career. You get real nervous, real tight, and then you screw up, just like Army did in tonight's game, by throwing a wild pitch in the tenth that allowed the winning run to score.

Now he's really in Billy's shithouse, and he's lucky if he ever gets to see the sun again. But, shit, Army's gotta be gettin' used to this shit. Since he was called up last month, he's only pitched about two innings, and I'm sure those were either in a game we were so far ahead that we couldn't have lost it even with him pitchin' or we were so far behind that Billy didn't want to use another pitcher.

Army's one of those guys that would view a trip to Columbus or anywhere else as a blessing. He's not doin' anything around here but driving himself crazy. The closest he gets to contributing anything to the club is in batting practice, where he is the most active shagger of fly balls I have ever seen in my life. If nothin' else, we should use him as a late-inning defensive replacement in the outfield. I've seen him make some unbelievable catches out there, running into walls for balls, and everything.

But when you come right down to it, Billy probably doesn't really care if Army shows up or not. And after tonight's game, he's probably gonna care even less.

Friday, June 21—DETROIT

Before or after a game, Billy can usually be the nicest guy in the world. But dress him up in the pinstripes, put him in the dugout, and he becomes all business. And fans seem to sense this, too. They can just sense how thin-skinned he is when he's managin' and they seem to get on his ass just that much more because of it.

Tonight was one of those cases. This guy behind the dugout was all over Billy's ass, like he'd paid the price of admission just to come and try to give ol' Billy the red ass. Well, tonight, he got his money's worth 'cause he got Billy's goat; yet, I think that Billy still got the best of him in the long run.

Billy put up with the guy's shit pretty well for the first few innings, until he just couldn't take it anymore and stepped out of the dugout, turned around to the guy, and said, "Hey, I think ya better go home and check on your wife. One of my players is missin'." I about died.

But today was just one of those rare days when Billy had the red ass after the game. After the game we were sittin' around in the hotel bar when a very good lookin' young lady came over and nicely asked him for his autograph. But bein' the little devil that he is, Billy thought she had some other, ulterior motive in mind, and he wasn't in the mood or had a headache or somethin' so he told her in his own rude way to leave.

Which really set this lady off. She just started screamin' at him at the top of her lungs, callin' him every name in the book, almost soundin' like Billy cussin' out an umpire. I guess Billy just brings that out in people.

Billy gave me six days off before this start and I was too strong again. I had no control over my knuckler and was walkin' guys left and right. So I had to go to the ol' number one more than I wanted to. But I was pretty lucky—until the sixth inning, that is, when the Tigers finally got me for four runs.

Then they added another one in the seventh and another one in the eighth, and we wound-up losin' 6–4. I'm now 7–6 on the season, and we dropped another game to Toronto in the standings. We're in fifth place, seven and a half games out. Right now, the Tigers, who are playin' great and who are only two and a half out, seem like the only team in the division which is capable of catchin' Toronto.

Saturday, June 22 — DETROIT

Guid saved somebody's job somewhere by breaking our losing streak, saving us from being swept and by shutting out the Tigers, 4–0. It was Guid's seventh consecutive victory and he seems to have fully regained his status as our stopper, which is exactly what we need. I just wish that I was doin' a better job of upholdin' my end. If I were, I'm sure we'd be at least a few games closer to the Jays.

Billy Gardner was fired today. Everything just seemed to kind of go downhill for him after Billy started gettin' on his shit. With all these firings, once again, I started to think that there may be more security in tryin' to be a forty-six-year-old big leaguer than in being a manager. I'll have to keep that in mind for when Ted calls.

Sunday, June 23 — DETROIT

The talk around here is that the club is planning on introducing somethin' called a Yankee hotline, where you can call a 900 number to get the details of the game and any news concerning the club. I'm sure it's only a matter of time before George makes it known around here that all Yankee employees, players, managers, and pitching coaches included, should begin calling in every morning to the hotline to see if they still have a job or not.

Shirls ruined his chances of becoming the American League Player of the Week for the second consecutive week, which would have crumbled the entire structure of this great game of ours, when Chet Lemon took him deep for a two-run shot, while Frank Tanana, who the Tigers just acquired, beat us 3–1. If this shit continues, Billy is gonna have to start phonin' that fuckin' hotline the first thing every morning, or when he gets in from his evening out, which is about the same thing.

Monday, June 24 — NEW YORK

Guid and Hendy were named as the American League's Co-Players of the Week. Guid pitched two shutouts to earn his half of the award, and ya kinda expect that from him. But you never expect a guy to hit .607, even if it's only for a week, which is what Hendy did.

I think all of us realized that he had the potential to be a great player, but I don't think any of us fully understood just how much he really possesses. This kid can do everything and he's real smart too. It usually takes a player a few trips around the league to learn how his club wants him to play certain hitters. For Hendy, it took only once through the lineup.

And he just loves the atmosphere and the crowds around here. He's kinda like one of those Yankees of old, who this atmosphere used to bring the best out of. He just loves it here. He's always lookin' into the stands at the fans whether it be during batting practice or a game.

In fact, he was voted, in our pregame meetings, as the Yankee most likely to be struck in the back of the head by a foul ball, while I was voted as the Yankee most likely to die on the mound.

Rags just hasn't been himself lately. And not wanting to risk losing a game to Weaver, Billy has been using Fish as our stopper until Rags gets it all back together, and Fish has responded well, as he did tonight.

But this one wasn't quite as easy as our last three wins against Baltimore. We had to score two in the bottom of the eighth to win this one, which probably just makes this victory that much sweeter for Billy, who just loves to frustrate the hell outta Weaver.

When Omar Moreno was with the Pirates, where he helped lead them to a World Series win in '79, he played in almost every game. And since he batted leadoff all the time, that usually meant that he led the league in at-bats.

So when Moreno was being shopped around as a free agent at the end of the '82 season, his agent thought that he should be rewarded for always being in the lineup. So he worked out some kinda at-bat clause in Omar's contract with Houston that formed a very big part of his yearly salary by paying him somethin' like $200 an at-bat.

Since Omar has come over here, with the exception of just a few weeks, he's been used almost exclusively as a late inning defensive replacement/pinch-runner, which basically nullifies his at-bat clause. Tonight he scored the winning run as a pinch-runner but didn't get any extra bucks for doin' so. But unfortunately he doesn't have a clause in his contract to cover that.

George is no dummy. Not only does he know how to make money, but he knows how to save it, too.

Shirls, our hero, who is 2–1 in his last three starts with a 2.08 ERA, is on his way back to the bullpen. But Shirls doesn't hold any grudges. He'll just be ready tomorrow for whatever role Billy decides to use him in. Every winning ball club needs a guy like Bob Shirley.

Tuesday, June 25 — NEW YORK

Whit is finally startin' to feel at home here, and Mark Connor, our pitching coach, has a lot to do with it. He's been workin' with Whit almost every day on his confidence and his approach to the game.

And ya can tell that Whit is startin' to enjoy himself more 'cause he's back to bein' himself, much to the dissatisfaction of Gene Michaels, our third base coach, who's legendary around here for being afraid of bugs and anything slimy, and a guy that Whit just loves to get on. Today, Whit said that he was goin' out before tomorrow's game to buy something slimy to put in Stick's boxer shorts. That's the old Whit that we know and love, and the one that the Yankees paid millions for.

Tonight, he was his old self on the mound, too. He wasn't dominating but he was good. A few weeks ago, without his newfound confidence and Connor's help, he would have lost this game somehow. But tonight he just had it in his mind that he was gonna win it and he did.

He was almost cocky out there tonight, like he expected to win. It was nice to see him back, even though I'm sure Stick might not fully agree. He allowed only one run through six and then turned the game over to the bullpen, which with our pen is almost always a sure save when you get that late in the game.

New lights were finally installed in the Metrodump. Billy may be unorthodox in his approach at times, but he does make himself heard.

Wednesday, June 26 — NEW YORK

They're havin' real attendance problems in Pittsburgh. Well, then, they always have. Even when the club was winning the pennant almost every year, the fans still never came out. It must be them goddamn unis. It'd be hard enough getting into one of those suckers, let alone being expected to pay to see someone else in one. No wonder the fans don't show.

Well, as somewhat of a last ditch effort to get the Pittsburgh fans to come out and show some sort of support (a crowd of at least 7,500 would be nice), the Pirates have arranged a Ballot-at-the-Ballpark Day outing on Sunday, in which the fans are supposed to show their support for the team by showing up on Sunday. I think the Bucs are even gonna let a few thousand fans in free.

In conjunction, the Pirates are supposed to be setting up all kinds of shit like concerts before and after the game, during the game, whatever, to attract fans, really givin' it their best effort. No money spared, mind you, so they decided to bring in half a dozen cows and set up a cow-milking contest before the game. Now, that may draw fans in Pittsburgh, but in New York that sucker would turn into a barbecue real quick.

After reading this shit in the paper today, I just realized how lucky I was that I didn't sign with the Pirates, or else I'd have found myself adorned in the ugliest uni in baseball.

It seems that even when we play shitty we can beat these Orioles. Rassy really got rocked early and lasted only one and two-thirds. But our relievers held 'em, and we came back and won it with two runs in the bottom of the ninth.

This is the sixth straight time that we've beaten Weaver's Orioles, and Billy is just lovin' it. Even if we don't win the pennant, if at least he can screw it up for Weaver, he will say that he had a successful season.

Thursday, June 27—NEW YORK

I was asked to testify in court today concerning a lawsuit by Topps Bubblegum Card Co. against some cheap impersonator or somethin'. In cases like this, they always like to call in the veterans first; and I guess I'm considered to be somewhat of a veteran's veteran, 'cause I'm always the first one called.

Well, anyway, as hotly as this thing was bein' contested, it was nothin' compared to spending a day in the pinstripes. In fact, this was probably the calmest part of the season for me so far, to me a day at the beach, a passive, quiet day spent relaxing in court.

Toronto's game against Milwaukee was the only game scheduled in the American League today. Toronto ended up beating the

Brewers, 7–3, which means that we dropped to six and one-half games behind 'em, approximately where we've been for the last three weeks.

Billy said that if we're within five games of 'em at the All Star break, he felt we'd have a good chance of winnin' the pennant. So he's expected to begin startin' a push around here any day now. So this'll probably be my last day at the beach. 'Cause from what I've heard, when Billy gets goin', things really start hoppin', as if they haven't been hoppin' so far. I just hope my forty-six-year-old psyche can handle it.

Friday, June 28 — NEW YORK

Guid was his usual self tonight, seven innings pitched, two runs allowed, eighth consecutive win. But the Jays beat the Tigers 2–0, so we didn't pick up any ground.

Rumors are startin' to circulate around here that George is tryin' to get either Neil Allen or Tommy John. We need starters, but I don't know if these guys are exactly what we're lookin' for.

Saturday, June 29 — NEW YORK

After pitching another poor game tonight, I think I've finally figured out my problem, 'cause it's just not like me to fold in the middle of a pennant race, especially when I'm feelin' as good as I am.

Ever since I admitted that, yes, I would be interested in returning to Atlanta, I think I've kinda been subconsciously sitting around waitin' for the phone to ring and for it to be George asking me if I'd O.K. a trade to Atlanta, or George calling to tell me that Ted had called to ask him if he could talk to me about becoming the new Braves manager.

I guess that that's been first and foremost in my mind lately and that's why I've been doin' so shitty. I feel terrible that it's been happenin', but I just didn't realize that it was happenin' until now, when I've already kinda given up hope about anything happenin'.

I thought that if somethin' was gonna happen, it would have happened by now. But it hasn't so I gotta get it off my mind and get my damn self together and worry about gettin' this club into the World Series.

But I think that even if I had been at my forty-six-year-old best tonight, I couldn't have beaten this kid Haas, who pitched a one-hitter, which is quite an accomplishment for anyone. But for a right-hander in Yankee Stadium, it's phenomenal.

Supposedly the deal with St. Louis for Allen was almost made, but then George insisted that the Cardinals take either Yog, Omar, or both as part of the deal. Now, if you were the Cardinals, which would you rather be stuck with: a $700,000-a-year back-up infielder who spends the majority of his time reading comic books; a $750,000-a-year, temperamental Panamanian pinch-runner; or a young, extremely highly paid pitcher, who at least still has a lot of pop in his arm? Right, that's why the Cards nixed the deal.

Walt Terrell of the Tigers is pitchin' like Cy Young. He shut out the Jays today and is already 9–3 this season. And just to think, we could've gotten him for Hendy, Mattingly, Guid, and Winnie. What a steal that would have been, huh?

Sunday, June 30 — NEW YORK

Billy wanted us to get our momentum goin' so bad for this upcomin' series with Toronto that he really fucked up today. To set the stage, Shirls started, looked horseshit, and lasted only one and two-thirds—back to bein' a hostage, maybe this time for good.

Then instead of bringin' in Bordi or Armstrong, one of his other hostages, Billy opted to bring in Fish instead, who's been our best short-reliever as of late. Then Billy left him in for five and one-third, which basically cooked him for the entire upcoming series with Toronto. Shit, the last time he went that long, it took him seven days to recuperate. He should have my job. It'd be perfect for him.

Well, anyway, Billy wanted this one real bad, too bad, and we wound up losin' it, which hurt us far worse than winnin' it could have possibly helped us. And as if things couldn't get worse, Toronto beat the Tigers again, sending us to seven and one-half back, which makes our upcoming series even more crucial, that is if we want to get as close as Billy wants to have us by the All Star break.

Billy, who knew that he screwed up, was totally into his defensive element after the game. With his trusty tape recorder at his side and with Joe Safety watching over all the goings on, Billy made it look like he was the Christian and the reporters were the lions.

About our only saving grace was that the Mets lost their fourth in a row, which gave Georgey a reason to smile and took some of the pressure off of us.

The Buccos ended up drawing only 31,000 on their Ballot-at-the-Ballpark Day.

It's not that I don't like the Pirates. It's just them goddamn uniforms. They just seem to bring out the worst in me. I suppose that may be the reason I've always pitched so well against 'em.

But, then, mom never liked 'em either, simply because they didn't sign me to a contract twenty-six years ago, when they had the chance, which would have made it real convenient for her and dad to see me play. But she still doesn't hate 'em as much as she's gonna hate George if she doesn't get her damn hats pretty soon.

Monday, July 1—TORONTO

It was Canada Day here today, whatever the hell that is. All I know is that I had to be at the ballpark about two hours before I usually get up, and thus I didn't really get enough time to sleep off the pains from my escapades of last night.

Thank God for Alka Seltzer. That stuff is a miracle cure. And I should know. I've been usin' it my entire career, and it hasn't failed me yet. Hell, I'd endorse that shit on TV for free just to thank the folks at Alka Seltzer for bein' such a constant contribution to my career. Hell, they've been as responsible as anybody, managers, coaches, other players included, for all the success I've had in my career.

The Jays got 41,000 for today's game. This is one of the best-supported teams in the majors. The fans up here have always been completely behind their team, even when the Jays were horseshit. They've been forced to endure hundreds of long losing streaks, several last-place finishes, and dozens of early season blizzards.

But then both Toronto and Montreal have always gotten the support they needed, whether they really deserved it or not. They've never had to have a tit-squeezin' contest to attract fans. No, sir. Instead, I think what keeps the Canadians coming back is their mutual affection for ale and for drinking it in the company of tens of thousands of their fellow countrymen.

They're also less critical and more faithful than American fans. It'll take 'em about forty losses in a row before they'll boo ya, and they even cheer long foul balls and an occasional good defensive play made by the opposition. The people up here just love to party and have a good time. It must be the fuckin' ale. The breweries must put something in the ale, somethin' that blurs their vision and dulls their senses so they can't always see what's goin' on on the field.

'Cause, believe me, they've had thousands of reasons to boo the players and the team down through the years. But they just keep comin' out. And this is not a boring town—believe me. There's a hell of a lot of other things goin' on besides baseball games. It must just be the ale. It's gonna make the Jays look better than they actually are. In fact, I guess you could go as far as to say that if there were any one person or thing that was responsible for savin' this franchise, it'd have to be the ale.

I guess that the only qualm I have with the two Canadian teams is that when the two franchises were initially admitted into baseball, their fans were just so un-American. Hell, they wouldn't even try to catch foul balls, no matter what.

In fact, they'd just treat the son of a gun like a hockey puck. We used to get the biggest kick outta watchin' the fans when baseball first came to Montreal. A foul ball would be hit into the stands and none of the fans would try to catch it. They'd just let it drop to the ground, then they'd all hop on it, like a fumble. I guess it must have just been their ice-hockey training, from here in the Yukon, which taught them to never use their hands when fielding anything.

But I must admit that they've gotten a hell of a lot better. No, they're still not catchin' all the balls, but they're tryin'. They still end up takin' quite a few off the forehead, nose, and chin, but they're tryin'.

Cowls started tonight and was great, and he'll continue to be great as long as they don't fool with him. He went eight and only gave up three hits and a run. Rags finished up and got his fourteenth save.

Donny got the big hit for us, a solo homer in the eighth, off of Doyle Alexander, that gave us a 2–1 lead. We added two more runs later in the game and wound up winning 4–1.

We're now within six and a half of the Jays, but we need to win all three games to really pick up any ground on these guys. 'Cause if we only win two out of three, then we only pick up one.

Alexander is the newest of the new knuckleball pitchers—what a trend setter I am. I hear that even Quisenberry is throwin' one now, but I consider that a little underhanded, if you know what I mean?

Well, Doyle, who's still bein' paid by George, has got all the qualifications, including a less-than-average fastball, to be a great knuckleball pitcher. In fact, Doyle's been playin' around with the knuckleball a little and used it quite a few times in our game today. I'm glad that for his sake he's seen the light, found the knuckler, and decided to let lady luck take over. And I bet his career will continue to prosper as a result.

It looks like Babe Hassey, as we now call him, is soon gonna lose his place in the lineup, 'cause Butch'll be comin' back off the Disabled List.

Surprisingly, or more like astonishingly, Hass has been our best hitter over the last few weeks. He's taken all that he's accomplished in his career up to this point and condensed it into a few weeks work. He's been phenomenal, especially when you consider his limited physical potential. In fact, about the only way you can tell that Hass is a pro athlete is he wears a uni. And even then, some of us look at him and question his choice of professions. He just doesn't look like a pro athlete.

But seeing him play gives youngsters a reason to continue following their dreams and leaves grown-ups, who gave up too early, wonderin' why they ever did so.

But there's one aspect of Hass that doesn't show up in his uni, and that's his heart. He's got as much heart as anybody on this team. That's the reason he's here.

Tuesday, July 2—TORONTO

Joe won No. 200 today by beating the Padres 3–2. I bought him a two hundred-year-old bottle of cognac and had it sent to him. I was gonna buy him a bottle of his favorite drink and have it sent to him, but try as I did I just couldn't come up with a two hundred-year-old bottle of Lite Beer.

Whit is really gettin' his game together. At the beginning of the season for some reason, he kinda nibbled around the hitters like they were laced with nitro or somethin'.

But now he seems to be back to his old ways. His confidence is back, thanks to Mark Connor, and he's challenging the hitters. We need him and we especially needed him today, and he came through for us, shutting down the Jays for eight innings as we walked away with a 5–3 win.

We're gettin' to where Billy wants us. We're only five and a half out, and I pitch tomorrow.

Billy just doesn't like Mike Armstrong for some reason, which just drives Army crazy. Today, a reporter asked Billy why he didn't use Army last Sunday against the Brewers, when we were low on pitchers and Fish had already pitched beyond his usual limit. Billy, quick on wit and long on vengeance, replied, "I was trying to win the game." No wonder Army's goin' nuts.

Wednesday, July 3—TORONTO

A few days ago Guid decided that he wanted to pitch at home against Minnesota on Thursday instead of here today against the

Jays. Which may sound strange, since we needed this one so badly. But when a guy is pitching as well as Guid, ya don't fool with him.

But when the story hit the papers, it caused all kinds of stink and the first guy interviewed was me, 'cause I had been chosen to take his place in the rotation. I, like everybody else, was a little confused by the whole thing and that's exactly what I told 'em. But in no way was I critical of Guid. I just never knew when the heck I was pitchin'. Some starts it's every nine days, sometimes four, this time three. I just never know when the hell I'm gonna start a game, which makes it real goddamn hard to prepare yourself. Shit, I'd just got used to pitching once a week, which is usually way too long in between starts for me, when Mark Connor came up and told me I was pitching today. So naturally my reaction was, "What the hell is goin' on?"

It's not that I was disagreeing with Billy's strategy or anything, I was just real confused, which is what I told the press. Unfortunately, they built it into one of their patented controversies, making me sound like a real back stabber and making Guid sound like he was chickening out of his start against the Jays.

When the real truth, as I found out later, was that Guid simply felt more comfortable starting at home, on grass and at night. Supposedly, he pitches better under those conditions. So Billy simply switched his start to Thursday and moved me back to today.

But it wasn't long before I caught hell from a group of Billy's lieutenants. That's just how things are communicated around here, never through a face-to-face meeting, but instead always through the messenger system.

Then Joe Safety was sent down to talk to me by someone in the front office. But Joe Safety of all people. That really hurt, havin' the PR man come over and tell ya something that whoever didn't have enough balls to tell ya himself.

Joe was just as embarrassed as hell, too, havin' to play the stooge and all. He's a class guy with a horseshit job. "I don't want to tell ya Knucks, I don't want to have to tell ya this, but I've gotta tell ya somethin' from you know who."

That sucks! Hearing that shit coming to me from a PR man.

Especially since all this wouldn't have happened and I wouldn't have been so fuckin' confused if everybody around here communicated with each other a little more openly.

I went in to see Billy about all that had happened and to explain what had gone on from my viewpoint. He was real calm, mild mannered, and polite, totally unlike a guy who would send his henchman out to shut up a guy.

I told him that nothin' I said was meant to come out in the papers as it did and that I wasn't tryin' to create any waves. I was just confused and was lookin' for some answers, that's all.

Like the fatherly—or as Baylor would say, fatherly-in-law— symbol that he is, he told me that he fully understood and to just watch what I said around the media from now on. And then he told me, "If too much more of this happens you should invest in one of these gadgets," and pointed to his handy-dandy cassette recorder, which he was still using to tape all his interviews.

I also stopped over to talk with Guid and told him that what I had said about him was taken half ass-backwards. Seemingly totally unaffected by the occurrences of the last few days, he said, "I've been around here too long to believe everything that's written in the papers."

Toronto scored first today with two in their half of the first, and I think that Billy was wonderin' if I'd ever get out of the inning. I think he wonders how I even get out to the mound sometimes. But I did. In fact, I felt real fine 'cause I prefer to pitch on four days rest, as I told Billy when he first got here, and three days rest is a whole lot closer to four days than the eight days that I had been pitching on.

But we came back and scored two off their ace, Dave Stieb, in the fifth to tie the game and eventually went to extra innings.

In the bottom of the tenth, with Bordi pitching, Toronto got their first two guys on base, first and second, when George Bell hit a soft roller to Pags at third, which was a tailor-made double-play ball.

But Pags, who we've just recently begun referring to as Rambo because of his aggressive style of play, instead tried to tackle Lloyd

Moseby, who was comin' from second to third. Moseby just gave Pags a head and shoulder fake and raced by him into third. Then Rambo just lost it, boundin' to his feet and throwing the ball miles over Donny's head at first and into the stands, allowing Moseby to score.

We left Toronto and headed home six and a half games back.

Thursday, July 4 — NEW YORK

Guid was his usual phenomenal self today. He shut down the Twins on six hits, as we won 3–2. It was Guid's ninth straight win and our eighth straight on the Fourth of July. A real patriotic bunch, that's us Yankees. We're all for everything that's American—the ol' stars and stripes, apple pie, and George.

One of the major reasons we've begun to play so well lately is that we've begun consistently to score first, which offers us a significant advantage in most cases.

Hendy has been our main reason for that. He's just like a blasting cap at the top of our lineup. He can hurt an opponent *sssooo* many ways, with his speed, with his power, and with his smarts.

Today, he and Griff, who's really been strugglin' because of some personal problems, led off the first with back-to-back singles and got things goin'. Then Mattingly doubled in one run and Hass was intentionally walked, the first of his career—sorry, just kiddin'. Then Baylor drove in two more with a duck fart to left, and all of a sudden we were up 3–0.

That's what a guy like Hendy can do for a ball club. And with the lineup we have, that's all we really need, just someone to get us started. Then once we get the ball rollin', we're pretty hard to stop. And with leads like that, it just makes our pitchers that much more relaxed and confident, and thus just that much more effective.

Some lady was shot at the game today. How it happened and who did it, no one really knows. I guess the lady was just sittin' there with her family watchin' the game when she heard this gun go off and then looked down and saw that her hand had a bullet hole in it.

But the police don't really have any clues as to who shot her. Some of the guys on the club kiddingly said that the girl that Billy cussed out in Detroit flew down here for the weekend hopin' to maybe get even. From what I hear, that's not the first woman to try and get even with Billy, only the first one today.

We picked up a full game in the standings on both Toronto and Detroit, who are both starting long West Coast road trips while we are just beginning a twelve game homestand against the remaining Western Division clubs, which we really clean up on here in the Bronx. So if there was ever a time to make up some ground, it'd be now.

Toronto's 3–2 loss to Oakland and Detroit's loss to Texas moved us within five and a half of the top and three away from the Tigers. Billy might just get his wish yet.

Friday, July 5 — NEW YORK

There are times when I dream of movin' back to Atlanta and playin' again for the Braves. Sometimes I wake up in the middle of the night and I can almost see the sights and taste the aromas of Atlanta. In fact, early this morning at about 4:00 A.M., I woke up from a dream and started vomiting, which is just about the time their game with the Mets ended last night. The son of a gun lasted nineteen innings, endured two rain delays, massive scoring slumps and was one of the most absurd feats in the history of sports.

No, sir, I sure as hell would not have wanted to be there for that one. And I don't know if my heart could have handled seeing Rick Camp, who'd be lucky to hit water if he fell out of a boat, hit his two-out, two-strike homer that tied the game and sent it into the eighteenth.

But not in old Atlanta. Hell, no. He hit the homer and the five thousand or so fans still left just started celebratin'. I heard a few of 'em even tried to tear down Hank Aaron's record breakin' No. 715 sign in left field and replace it with a tribute to Camp, who some of these crazies supposedly started to worship as a hero.

Then I heard that after the Mets finally came to their senses and scored three in the nineteenth, the Braves were jugglin' their line up every way possible to try and get Campy up just one more time.

Hendy did it again. This time he led off the first with a double and immediately the team caught fire and wound up scoring three in the first. In the second, Hendy led off with his eleventh homer of the season and Griff followed with his fourth, and we were out to a 5–1 lead.

It's good to see Griff comin' around. He's just such an inspiration for us when he's playin' good, especially when we all know about how he's dealin' with a lot of real tough personal problems at home.

The early lead really helped Rassy, who's been pitchin' real bad lately. Somebody must be messin' with his head. 'Cause anybody with stuff as good as his couldn't be pitchin' as bad as he is for any other reason.

He's also had a lot of tough no-decisions so far this season, and they weigh heavy on a young pitcher's mind. But tonight was kind of a confidence booster for him. He didn't pitch that well and only lasted five and a third, but he won and that's all that mattered.

Toronto beat the A's 8–2, so we didn't pick up any ground on them. But at least we gained a game on Detroit who lost to Charlie Hough and Texas 3–1.

Saturday, July 6 — NEW YORK

Sometimes the most absurd of things will help in this game, such as the Indian medicine man that George hired from Fort Apache, here in the Bronx, to come over and do a rain dance around the pitchers mound after the Twins took an early 6–2 lead.

Shortly after, the sky just literally opened up and the umps ended up callin' the game. Ray Miller, the Twins' new manager, who's used to playin' in the Metrodump, just went wild. Sorry, Ray, see ya tomorrow. Thank God for Yankee ingenuity!

It seems that every time a Yankee writes one of these books his ass is gone the next season. Billy wrote his book and was fired. But then what's new? Sparky Lyle wrote *The Bronx Zoo* and was traded to Texas the season after. And Graig Nettles wrote *Balls* and was later traded to San Diego. I wonder what miracle this sucker will work for me?

The magic of these publications is well-known and well-respected around the Yankee clubhouse. In fact, when Griff first stated that he wanted to be traded so badly in the beginning of the season, several guys told him just to write a book. "It works every time," they said.

There's some question whether that procedure now works in reverse, though, meaning that writing a book after leaving the Yanks may get you sent back here. That's what is keepin' Nettles from doin' a sequel to *Balls*. According to Graig: "The last time I wrote a book, I got traded from the East Coast to the West Coast. I'm afraid they'd send me back if I wrote another." I'll have to keep that in mind.

Sunday, July 7—NEW YORK

Tricky Dick Nixon was at the doubleheader today. I guess that since Nixon has left his obscure little hideout on the West Coast and decided to rejoin the political world, he's taken to living here in New York and thus has become a Yankee fan. He's at several of our games and even shows up on the road sometimes. No wonder we have so many leadfoots followin' us around all the time.

Don Mattingly's errorless streak ended at 153 games today when he bobbled a ground ball in the first game. Donny is just phenomenal. With the exception of pissin' behind an occasional dumpster or two, he carries a lot of maturity for his age. Heck, I've taken leaks right in the middle of a crowded barroom before. It's just hard to believe that he's only twenty-four years old.

It's also hard to believe that with all the seasoned veterans that we've got, Donny's the one we really look to for leadership. He just never lets down, no matter what the score or the situation. We could be down by ten in the ninth and he'd still be out there bustin' his ass which kinda has a residual effect. Nobody ever lets down because of him. You can't, you'd just be too embarrassed to do so.

So when any of us are feelin' down, we just glance over at Donny and get our batteries recharged. More than anyone else on this team, he exemplifies what bein' a Yankee is supposedly all about.

Ray Miller was really steamin' today after we swept his team in the doubleheader. He's just gotta learn that there's nothin' that money can't buy, including a rainout.

Hendy and Griff were again the stars. But in the first game, it was Winnie's home run in the tenth that won it for us. As usual, we scored in the first inning in both games. It's becoming a tradition around here.

Whit started the first game and pitched pretty well, but we couldn't get him more than two runs until the tenth, and by that time Rags was in the game and got credit for the win.

In the second game, Hendy scored two runs and Griff hit two singles, as we once again scored in the first and then went on to a 14–2 victory. I think that by that time the Twins had already given up. I just think they thought there was no way they were gonna beat us, especially after George got away with the medicine-man stuff the other night.

I guess the highlight of the second game was that Army, makin' his first appearance in a game since the last passing of Haley's Comet, got in and pitched two shutout innings of relief. A 14–2 lead, Billy sure knows how to pick just the right spot to use each one of his pitchers.

Billy has finally given up platooning Dale Berra, who's just been a bundle of nerves with all that drug stuff in Pittsburgh, at third with Pags.

And just to think, Billy was the one who recommended that the Yanks go after Yog. But now, after seeing Yog play for themselves, some folks around here think that Billy may have made his recommendation after spending quite a few innings in the press lounge downing drinks.

Toronto won again yesterday and so did Detroit. But since we swept the doubleheader, at least we picked up a half a game on both of 'em. We're now four and a half back of Toronto and two back of the Tigers.

Monday, July 8 — NEW YORK

The other night I was sittin' around after the game, gettin' ready to go out and I turned on the tube. The David Letterman show was on. As I was gettin' dressed, I was kinda half listenin' when I heard Letterman start rippin' on my old buddy from the Braves, Terry Forster. I couldn't believe it! Letterman started callin' him "a fat tub of goo," "a silo" and "a balloon." I just couldn't believe it. His descriptions of Terry were just so accurate. As I listened to Letterman, I could just see this vision of Terry appearing before my eyes.

He must know Terry or somethin', or otherwise he wouldn't have been able to describe him so well. As Letterman said, Terry's just too big to be a baseball player, too big to be anything for that matter, with the exception of maybe a side of a barn. That's Terry alright. The guy just lives to consume pizza, beer, and tacos. If Dominos Pizza were allowed to deliver to the Braves bullpen, they'd double their sales in one year, just based on Terry's purchases alone. Heck, the guy doesn't sweat when he gets into a game, he foams.

But after hearing all this shit, even though it was true, I was just wonderin' how Terry was takin' all this, comin' out on national TV and all that. So I called Nancy, who said she had talked to Terry's wife already. She said that at first Terry was so pissed off he was gonna sue Letterman, but then on the way to the telephone to call his attorney, he passed by a mirror, took a good look at himself and realized that Letterman was right.

Letterman, who I think is somewhat of a baseball fan, just loves to do shit like that. In fact, at the beginnin' of the '84 season when I was rippin' off one victory after another, Letterman called the Yanks and asked if I'd come on his show. Since I'm always willing to do anything for the club (I guess even that), I decided to go on with him.

When I walked out on stage, I found Letterman standing there with a catcher's mitt. He wanted me to toss him a few knucklers so the viewing audience could see just how this mystical sucker that I throw moves. So he squatted down, and I tossed him a few easy ones, as I tried to loosen up my arm.

Then he began eggin' me on by sayin', "*Aww* come on, can't you throw any harder than that?" So right then and there I tried to do what *sooooo* many Terry Forsters had wanted to do for *sooooo* long. I grooved a pitch right for Letterman's love nest.

We didn't score in the first inning tonight. In fact, Kansas City did and went on to beat us 5–2.

I took the loss, and even though the loss was my fifth straight, I really didn't pitch that bad. I went the distance, walked four and allowed only four earned runs. The knuckler was movin' today like I wish it had moved on Letterman's show, right into their nuts.

But we just couldn't hit this Saberhagen kid that they threw out there. He's a real tough son of a gun. And at his age, twenty-one, he's supposed to be frightened by teams like us.

We just had a hard time gettin' anything goin' off the kid, except in the seventh when one of the weirdest plays I'd ever seen took place. Well, I guess I should be used to that shit here in the Bronx, but I'm not.

We were trailin' by a score of 4–2 at the time, and Baylor stepped to the plate and scorched a ball down the third-base line, past George Brett. But then the umpire throws up his hands to stop play. Then the ump walks over to where a small blue ball was layin' on the infield, holds it up and says that it interfered with Brett's attempt to make the play. Nullify Baylor's double, nullify everything.

I could have sworn that I saw Brett laugh, then take the ball from the umpire and put it back in his back pocket. Just kiddin'. But one thing Brett does know about is playin' here. Hell, he was part of enough losin' league championship teams here that he oughta know how to win. And today the Royals did win, their first here since the Great Pine Tar controversy back in '83. I was just glad that I could be a part of it all.

Omar refused to go into the game yesterday as a pinch-runner, 'cause he said his back hurt. How the heck could that have happened? The son of a gun hasn't done anything but pinch-run in months?

So Billy told him to come to the park early today to get treatment. Omar showed up three hours late. So Billy and George had a meeting with him, and George said after the meeting, "I think he's gonna be so cooperative from now on that the world won't believe it."

But Omar had a totally different interpretation of what went on. "Nothing's new. I have got nothing to say." Obviously, something must have gotten lost in translation.

Lou Piniella came up to me before the game to tell me that he had heard that the Braves had been in contact with George about reacquiring me. Shit, why now? Why when I had just gotten my mind off all that shit and got it back to the pennant race? Screw it, I may dream about it, but I'm not gonna let it influence how I pitch. 'Cause there's nothin' more important to me at this time than this pennant race.

Detroit lost to Chicago but Toronto won again by shutting out Seattle. We're back to five and a half back again. Catchin' those suckers may be harder than we originally thought.

Tuesday, July 9 — NEW YORK

That lady that got shot at the game last week is real ticked off at George. Today in the newspaper, she called him "callous and ignorant." Sounds like she's been speakin' to some of his ex-players.

Even though Guid was not at his best, he was still good enough to win. He worked eight and two-thirds and gave up nine hits, but only two earned runs, for his tenth win in a row.

Then Fish and Rags came in and shut 'em down. Right now, I can't think of a better rightie-leftie combination in the big leagues than those two.

Toronto won another over Seattle, this one with a five-run outburst in the thirteenth. I think we've tended to underestimate the drive and enthusiasm of their club. We think that since they're young, inexperienced, and from Canada, they'll fold. Bullshit! These guys have guts.

Last night their catcher, Buck Martinez, broke his ankle trying to block the plate, but still had the balls to try and tag out the next guy tryin' to score, before he passed out from the pain. Now that's balls.

The Tigers won, too. They scored four in the bottom of the ninth against the White Sox to do so. So we're still five behind Toronto and two back of Detroit.

It's interesting to watch these guys from our union and the owner's reps go at it. Unfortunately, though, they're playin' with my future and the future of this game.

A few months ago, the owners came out and said that they estimated their losses for '84 would be somethin' like $43 million. Today, the accountant who came up with that figure said that he had overestimated by $16 million. Only $16 million!

Today, both sides are scheduled to meet for somethin' like the thirty-first time since our contract ran out last year. What the hell do they do at those meetings. Hell, that's more times than I've seen my wife since I've moved here. And one thing for sure, Nancy and I get something accomplished every time we get together.

But what the heck do they do. I think they're just playin' around with each other. In fact, if it was up to me, I'd lock 'em all in one room with no food, no water. Then if they hadn't reached a decision by a certain time, I'd throw George in there with 'em. He'd get this thing over with real quick. He may fuck it up, but he'll get it over with real quick.

Wednesday, July 10 — NEW YORK

There's a lotta things that go into makin' up a winning ball club and one of 'em is attitude. Dave Winfield, though he sometimes gets overlooked, has the attitude of a winner and the physical abilities to go along with it.

But he often doesn't get any of the credit that he deserves. Most fans just see him as an awesome physical structure who is paid more than adequately for what he does. But his teammates know better than that. For in his own way, Winnie is as much a part of the heart and soul of this club as any guy wearin' the pinstripes. And he adds a dimension that no one else can, not Guid, not Willie, not Mattingly, Baylor or me.

Winnie's our challenger. He challenges us to win, to be better than we presently are.

Today Hendy came into the clubhouse limpin' real bad from the ankle he sprained in last night's game. From the way he was walkin', it didn't look like there was gonna be any way that he'd be in the lineup tonight.

But Dave, knowin' how important Hendy is to our team, went over and worked some of his magic on him. When the lineup was announced before the game, Hendy's name was on it.

Then with the score tied 5–5 in the bottom of the ninth, Hendy led off the inning with a single and immediately stole second. Then, after Griff popped up, Donny was intentionally walked, sending Winnie to the plate. Just then a note flashed on the scoreboard: DAVE WINFIELD HAS EIGHT GAME-WINNING RBIs.

Winnie smiled confidently and said to the ump, gesturing toward the scoreboard, "That's soon gonna be nine." And a few pitches later, it was. Not only did Winnie win the game for us with his game-winning hit, but he also set it up by talkin' Hendy into playing. Winnie challenges us, he challenges himself, and we're a far better team because of it.

That lady that got shot is suing George for $50 million, for what she calls "willful disragerd for human safety."

Both Toronto and Detroit won again. We're not gainin' as quickly or as much on this homestand as we thought we would.

Thursday, July 11—NEW YORK

Today's game was just one of those crazy games that ya get every once in a while, the kinda fun ones that shake things up a little.

We were playin' the Texas Rangers, who always seem to play us like they're playin' for their lives, which they probably are. There's just not that much else for a team like the Rangers to play for.

Everything all started when this rookie they had pitchin' for 'em, named Glen Cook started buzzin' our guys. In the first inning, he hit Hass in the leg, which will literally slow him down to a crawl now. Then, in the second, he plunked Meach in the head.

Well, ya know how Billy is. He takes that shit real personal, like you were actually throwin' at him or somethin'. So he goes out and tells Cowls to retaliate, which he does by plunkin' Curtis Wilkerson. It's a war now!

The next batter is Toby Harrah, who we traded to Texas for Billy Sample. Like most refugees of the organization, Harrah dislikes how he was handled here. As a result, he has this intense dislike of anything in pinstripes.

So Cowls got Harrah to ground to Donny at first, who tossed back to Cowls, who was racin' over to cover the bag when Harrah body-blocked him. Cowls got up with a big gash on his nose and blood all over his face. Now, I'm not sure if that took balls or a lot of stupidity on Harrah's part, 'cause one thing ya gotta remember is that poor teams don't have the capabilities to vent their frustrations in a worthwhile manner. Good teams do.

We came back and kicked their asses the next inning with eight runs.

Toronto won again. They beat California 5–3. Shit, they're beatin' everybody. But Detroit got beat by Minnesota in the Metrodump, so at least we picked up a game on them.

Friday, July 12 — NEW YORK

The Rangers oughta know better than to fool with us by now. We really came out and kicked their asses again.

As usual, we scored in the first inning. Mattingly was our big hitting star. He went three for three and knocked in three runs, using all three fields.

Whit shut out the Rangers on only four hits. There's been such a change in Whit; but then there's been quite a change in all of us. Comin' to the ballpark is the highlight of our days. We're playin' happy, playin' tough, and are in the pennant race. Could we ask for anything more? It's just when Whit quits sabotaging Stick's boxer shorts that I'll start to worry. Until then, I'll just go with the flow.

Dan Pasqua was recalled from Columbus today. The kid failed miserably in his first trip up here this spring though we all know he's got great talent. He was feelin' the pressure too much.

But tonight Pasqua started in right field for Winnie, who had to fly home for a funeral, and he ended up hitting two dingers into the upper deck. This kid may just turn out to be the next Mickey Mantle, as long as they don't fool with him. But I guess that there'll be almost no chance of that, so I just hope he learns to handle the pressure better.

According to the newspaper, some crazy lady stripped to her G-string the other night in the Cardinals game in San Francisco and left the park without taking her clothes home.

Both the Jays and the Tigers lost last night, which means we're now tied with Detroit for second place, five games behind Toronto, or exactly where Billy wanted us to be by the All Star break.

Saturday, July 13 — NEW YORK

I was takin' a lot of shit today because it was Old Timers Day.

It all started when I got to the ballpark. Usually for these things, the players are asked to share their lockers with the old-timers. But when I got to the park I noticed that I was the only guy using my locker, while everybody else was sharin' theirs. So I asked our clubbie why. He answered without even crackin' a smile, "I figured that with you usin' it there was both an old-timer and a Yankee usin' it already."

The Old Timers game is big around here. When ya look in the players' eyes, as they see all their boyhood heroes appear before them, it looks like you're lookin' into the eyes of a twelve-year-old. I feel the same way. God, I feel like a forty-year-old again, bein' around these guys.

Some of the guys even brought in balls, bats, and cards to have autographed. Mark Connor brought in his camera and was gonna take some pictures of the guys on the field before the game. That was, of course, until George started foolin' with him.

Mark was in the dugout takin' pictures of the guys on the field when George called him and started screamin' at him over the phone about how he was gettin' fined $250 for wearing his hat backwards. You could just hear old George screaming at him right through the phone.

"I'll tell you one damn thing. The next time I see you with your hat on like that, you're gonna be the pitchin' coach in fuckin' Watertown, New York."

I felt real embarrassed and bad for Mark, who spent the rest of the afternoon in the clubhouse mopin'.

As I guess was appropriate with the Old Timers game and all, I was scheduled to start against the Rangers, who've become a real pain in the ass for me.

Like everybody else, I was all psyched up from the festivities, so I started the Rangers out with my best heat, all sixty-five miles per hour of it, and I shut 'em down in order for the first three innings. Shows ya how bad they are.

Then I decided to mix things up a little the second time through their lineup, so I switched to some real slow shit, and I mean real slow shit. The only thing keepin' this shit off the grass was an updraft.

The slowest shit I threw was the slip pitch, which I hadn't thrown in years but decided to dust off for this game, kinda my way of celebratin' the return of the old-timers and my way of impersonating them also. I originally learned the slip pitch, which resembles what's used in slow pitch softball, from Ron Reed back in 1969. I'd just had the best year of my career, winning twenty-three games, and Paul Richards, who was the Braves' GM at the time, said I could've won even a few more games if I'd had a slip pitch. So he sent me down to the instructional league to work on one. But I never got to feelin' very comfortable with it until several years later, and by that time they wouldn't let me use it.

So I just kinda screwed around with it occasionally in the bullpen. That was until I got here of course, and Yog pretty much gave me a free rein on what I threw. So I decided to try and mix it into my repertoire, but I didn't decide to actually use it until today.

The first guy I used it against was Toby Harrah, who's been really pumped up for this series. So he comes up to the plate lookin' for a fastball and swingin' from his ass. When I tossed that sucker to Harrah, his eyes got real big and he about shit himself when he swung at it.

Billy kinda gave me a strange look out of the corner of his eye from the dugout, as if to say, "I don't like it, but if it gets the suckers out, go ahead and use it."

The next guy I used it on was this kid named Dunbar. I got behind on him real fast, and I knew that he'd be just sittin' back waitin' on my heater, so I threw him my old slipper. The son of a bitch caught him totally by surprise. Strike two!

So Butch called for the son of a gun again, and this time ol' Dunbar literally screwed himself into the ground tryin' to hit it, and ended up just foulin' it off. Then I came back with a third, which totally baffled him and just left him walking back to the dugout shakin' his head.

But the guys on our bench looked almost as surprised as Dunbar. They thought I was impersonating the old-timers or something. In a way I was, 'cause I figured if DiMagg and Mantle and greats like that have a hard time hitting this shit, then why wouldn't it work on guys like Harrah and Dunbar?

We won the game 3–1. I went seven innings and pitched the best that I had in a long time. Career victory No. 292.

When I got in the clubhouse, my son John, who'd flown up for the weekend, was walkin' around kinda lost, so I walked up to him and asked him what was the matter.

"I've been lookin' everywhere for ya," he said.

"Well, I was pitchin', son."

"You were pitchin' now, dad?"

"Ya, I just got finished pitchin', why?"

"Oh, that explains why I couldn't find ya. The guys around here told me you were pitchin' the first game today."

Sometimes, you can't even trust your own son.

. . .

California finally beat the Blue Jays, so we picked up another game on 'em. Now we're only three and a half back with one more game left to play before the break.

Billy's lookin' real happy, but then he should be. We're ahead of the pace he set for us a month ago, and he and his old buddy Mickey Mantle have been running together the last few nights.

Those two are the best of friends, legends not just in the hearts of faithful Yankee fans but in the minds of bartenders everywhere. These two are just as close, if not closer, than they were as players. The other night they asked me if I wanted to tag along with 'em. "*Heellll* no," I said. "I'm too old to try to keep up with you guys. For that matter, so are guys even as young as Mattingly and Meach."

Whitey Ford was in town for the Old Timers game too. He seemed a little worried about Mick's health. I guess he's got a spot on his lung or somethin'. So Whitey tries to keep a pretty close eye on him.

But I saw Whitey smilin' the other day, as he stood by his locker, watchin' Billy and Mick play around together before the game. He said it was the best he'd seen Mick ever look after spendin' five days with Billy.

I'd have to say that Mick's gonna be O.K., too. Hell, if he can keep up with Billy, he can run a marathon. I should know. I've only played for the guy for the last few months and already I feel like I've aged thirty years. Hey, maybe that's why I've been pitchin' like I was seventy five?

The Braves set up a special telephone number in Atlanta for fans to call and have recorded any special memories they may have of my career. It's all part of the day they're plannin' on havin' for me in September.

I was talkin' to Nancy the other day and asked her if she had called in yet?

"No," she said.

Love makes us all wise guys.

Sunday, July 14 — NEW YORK

Bill Madden of the *Daily News* wrote his usual column in the paper today, in which he asked players what grade they would give themselves for their performance so far this season.

Me, I gave myself an *F*. I've been pitchin' inconsistently. And after all that shit I took yesterday from the players, the old-timers, my kid, and my wife, I thought it was the only grade I deserved.

Omar was the only player that didn't participate. Madden marked him down as being absent.

We won again today and finished this half in the middle of a winning streak. The win was Guid's eleventh in a row. He just literally blew the Rangers away today with fastballs, and he wound up throwing only ninety pitches. Shit, I throw that many in three innings.

The win drew us within two and a half of the Jays, who lost again to California. I heard that Billy was so happy that he was gonna go out with Mick tonight and have a few drinks.

Thursday, July 18 — MINNESOTA

Leaving home was real hard, but when I left I kinda felt that it would be the last time that I'd ever have to come home for an All Star break after being away for so long and then have to go away again. At least according to the newspapers, it'd probably be the last time I'd ever have to do so.

But any bad feelings I had about leaving Nancy and the kids behind, I quickly forgot once I got to the ball park, where Billy was ranting and raving around the clubhouse like a wildman. I guess that he was really pissed off at both Sparky Anderson and Nolan Ryan. Anderson because Billy felt that he had deliberately left Hendy, who's still sufferin' from a bad ankle, in the game too long. Billy and George supposedly even sent a letter in to the league office requesting that Hendy be used as little as possible. Sparky left him in six innings.

But in Sparky's defense, he asked Hendy how he felt after Hendy'd been in only three innings, and Hendy said that he felt fine. Then Anderson asked him if he wanted to stay in and Hendy said that he did. So what's Anderson supposed to do then? Take him out? Hell, no! He wanted to win the goddamn game, and the best way to do so is to go with your best players. And Hendy is definitely one of the best players in baseball.

To be perfectly honest, I don't think Anderson did anything deliberate. I just think that Billy has a problem with persecution. But then who wouldn't have after being fired as many times as he has been?

As far as Billy's squabble with Ryan, I guess that stems all the way back to 1977 when Billy chose Frank Tanana as the starting pitcher for the All Star Game instead of Ryan. Since then, the feuds been goin' fast and furious, with Billy constantly fanning the fire by calling Ryan a .500 pitcher every chance he gets.

So when Ryan knocked both Hendy and Winnie down, Billy felt that was really meant for him. And it probably was, but why the heck does Billy always have to antagonize guys with ninety-eight-mile-per-hour fastballs. Why can't he just fool with guys like me and Charlie Hough?

We got Metrodumped tonight. But this time it wasn't the lights that got us, but instead the damn artificial turf. Shit, droppin' a baseball on this stuff is like dropping a superball onto a concrete driveway out of a plane flying at thirty thousand feet.

In the first inning, Kirby Puckett led off with a hit that began as a slow roller toward Pags at third and ended up into a ultra-high bounder that even Wilt Chamberlain, in his prime, couldn't have corralled. Puckett's hit eventually led to a two-run lead for the Twins in the first.

Then, in the second, whoever was leading off hit another high hopper that led to two more runs, and Whit was gone real quick.

Though we miraculously later tied the score, Kent Hrbek hit a legitimate grand slam in the seventh off of Fish, who I think Billy now sees as his stopper (or at least before tonight, he did), that put the Twins on top for good.

Since the A's handed the Jays their fourth straight loss, we failed to pick up another game, but at least we didn't lose one either. Detroit also lost, which should make Billy, who's still really pissed at Anderson, really happy. So happy that he may even go out and celebrate tonight.

George finally picked up Neil Allen from the Cardinals. I think that Billy wanted him more than anyone, though. I think he envisions him as the next great Yankee reliever. Or at least he hopes he will be; that way he can put Rags back in the starting rotation.

But for as horseshit as Allen has been pitchin', it still took quite a bit to get him. The Cards just wouldn't take Omar and Yog. No way. They wanted to get rid of Allen and they were willing to give him away. But no way they were gonna get stuck with two of our stiffs.

Friday, July 19 — MINNESOTA

I heard that Billy was so pissed off about losin' last night's game on those damn moon hops that he was considerin' holdin' a special practice session for us today in a weightless room, the kind they use to train astronauts in, but that he couldn't find one.

Either way, we played better ball tonight. Cowls pitched a good game for the first five and two-thirds, then Bordi and Rags shut 'em down the rest of the way, and we ended up winning 6–4.

Baylor got fined $100 for hitting a two-run homer tonight because he didn't look down to Stick to get the sign. Shit, it was a 3–0 pitch, and he's been makin' a pretty good livin' over the last fifteen years hittin' in that situation. So why should he look down? Stick gave him the green light anyway.

Mom called today about the hats again, and I used the opportunity to tell her about that number in Atlanta, (404) 976-PHIL, in case she wanted to call in with anything. Then she asked me, "Who's Phil?"

. . .

Toronto beat Oakland 5–1, so we're still two and a half back. But Detroit lost. It's gonna be hard to keep Billy in after he hears that news.

Saturday, July 20 — MINNESOTA

Whit invited me to go fishin' with him and the Twin's equipment man, a guy named Randy, today. They had a fishin' hole picked out already and everything. But as soon as I got there I found out that Whit was havin' about as much luck fishin' this year as he was pitchin'.

I caught a few fish right off and so did Randy, while Whit hadn't even gotten a nibble. So after a while, I said to myself, "Screw it, I don't want to embarrass Whit, so I'll just reel in and sit here and drink a few beers until Whit catches his first one." A case or so later, Randy, who'd decided to do the same thing, finally pulled up anchor and took us back to shore.

Billy has transformed us. We're smart, we're aggressive, and we're havin' fun. Never have I seen this type of spirit on a ball club before. Right now we're playing like we're all one out there, same uniform, same goal, same hangover.

When we go out there now, we expect to win, and I can't ever remember havin' as much fun at any time in my career as I'm havin' now. I'm proud to be a part of this whole thing and I'm proud to be a Yankee. That's just the kind of pride and respect that Billy breeds. I don't give a shit what's written about him. When you're playin' for him, he treats you like a man. No curfews or nothin', and you play better for it.

Tonight, Guid won his twelfth straight game. The last time he lost a game was all the way back in April, on Billy's first day. As usual, he was phenomenal. He just mowed down the Twins like they were standing still.

Hendy and Donny keyed the offense for us. As usual, Hendy got us goin' in the first inning and we wound up scoring four runs. Hendy finished the evening with three hits in five at-bats. Donny drove in four runs with a double and a dinger. The Jays lost to Oakland, so we're now only one and a half from the top spot.

Sunday, July 21 — MINNESOTA

The momentum on this ball club is contagious. There's a fever goin' around the clubhouse. Guys are walkin' around pumpin' each other up before ball games. It's like a nice disease.

Today, Winnie staked me to a 3–0 lead in the first with a 456-foot, three-run homer, the longest dinger ever to be hit in this park. That was basically all the help I needed, as I came within four outs of becomin' the oldest pitcher in big-league history ever to pitch a shutout.

They say that I'm a few days older than Satchell Paige was when he pitched his last shutout. Horseshit! As far as I'm concerned, nobody's older than ol' Satchell, not even Billy. The forty-six years old he said he was on that day was just the figure that popped into his mind. Nobody knows how old Satchell was when he pitched that sucker.

But it wasn't just me and Winnie out there today. Hell, no! It was a total team effort, like it is every day. Guys were divin' for balls, crashing into walls, and slappin' each other on the back all day. Billy has really got us playin'.

Monday, July 22 — KANSAS CITY

Butch hurt his back today and was put on the fifteen-day D.L. Poor Butch, he's been having a real tough year. First, he gets beaned in the head and spends a few nights alone in the hospital with visions of Billy and George floating around his head, and now this.

Safety put together a press release today saying that Dom had been activated to take his place. Safety put George's signature on it and everything. Dom just about shit.

He fell for the whole thing, hook, line, and sinker. Within minutes he was talkin' about gettin' out of the jewelry business that he uses to help support himself. Then he started complainin' to Safety about his name not bein' on the damn All Star Game roster. We just laughed our asses off.

Rassy started for us tonight and was sailin' along pretty good until about the fourth, when Cowls, who was listening to the audio hook-up of the ABC game in the dugout, told him that Cosell had just said that he was gone if he didn't turn in a good outing tonight. Rassy nearly went into shock. Nobody had said anything to him about it, and he just couldn't believe that Cosell was announcing this shit all over the country. So he goes out there after hearing all this shit and gets his brains beat in. Then when he gets into the clubhouse, the TV is on and he hears Cosell say that he's probably gone. Yet, still no one has talked to him. What a way to find out.

I was real pissed off about the whole thing so I went over and asked Mark Connor what the hell was goin' on, and he said that neither he or Billy knew anything about it.

We ended up losin' the game, as K.C. scored five in the fifth off of Rassy. Toronto beat Seattle 3–1, so we dropped to two and a half games back.

Tuesday, July 23 — KANSAS CITY

By the time that Rassy got to the park today, his bags were already packed for him. Billy didn't even know anything about it, and he was really pissed. All he knew was that when he got to the park, Marty Bystrom was there and Rassy was on the way out.

What a time for something like this to happen. I mean how did Cosell know about this in the first place, anyway. And who authorized Rassy being sent down. Maybe all this had something to do with Cosell sitting with George in his booth before the game? It sure wasn't Billy, 'cause he was just as surprised as anyone. I thought Billy was supposed to be in on all these moves anyway? I guess not. I guess that when it comes to certain aspects of this ball club, like choosing who's on his team, he's just a pawn too.

I feel bad for Rassy too. Somethin' like this could really screw up his head for a long time.

We lost again today. Whit took the loss. This kid the Royals have, Saberhagen, looked great again. He's real mature for his twenty-one years. He also doesn't have anyone foolin' with him, like Rassy does.

The Jays won again, so we're now three and a half back. At least we're not sinking alone, 'cause Detroit lost again too.

Wednesday, July 24 — KANSAS CITY

There's talk floatin' around that George is thinkin' about signing Carlton Fisk at the end of the year as a free agent. Fisk, who was big in the beginning, has really added a whole hell of a lot of extra bulk. He's massive.

I can just see it now, the Yankees new all-mean infield, featuring the Hulk behind the plate and Rambo at third. That'd be George's kinda team. A team that would demand respect.

We lost again, and Toronto won. We're now four and a half back and fallin' quick.

Frank White was the hero tonight for the Royals. Cowls started for us and was terrible. I don't know what's the matter with him, but he seems to have lost all his confidence. I think it may all have to do with what happened to Rassy the other night.

Thursday, July 25, OFF DAY — TEXAS

Toronto won again. They beat California 7–0. We're now five back. Detroit won, too, and they're now only a game and a half behind us, and Boston is only a game behind them.

Friday, July 26 — TEXAS

You know we're really goin' bad when Guid doesn't win, and you know we're goin' even worse when he gets his ass kicked by the Texas Rangers. But he didn't get the loss, Rags got that when his wild pitch allowed the winning run to score in Texas' five-run eighth.

It was a shame that we lost, too, 'cause we just kept battlin' back. Texas took the early lead, but we came back with three in the fourth to go ahead. Then we scored four in the fifth and another in the eighth. But their five-run eighth just killed us.

Harrah, of course, was their hero. He went three for four, scored three runs, and drove in another two. Down here, where they seem to just despise us, he's their hero because he's beating us more than anybody.

Of course, Toronto won again, so we're now six games back.

We've dropped four-and-a-half games in the standings in a week. There'll be hell to pay for this. You can bet on that. In fact, Billy thought that it'd be best if we all called the Yankee Sportsphone before leaving for the park tomorrow to make sure that they were still expectin' us.

Saturday, July 27—TEXAS

It's never bothered me to talk to reporters on the day that I pitch. In fact, I see it as part of my job. But some guys, in fact most starting pitchers, say that it breaks their concentration if they talk to reporters before they pitch, which is just a bunch of bull.

It's just their way of gettin' out of doin' any interviews for a day. And because most owners fall for this bull, they stand by their pitchers' request not to do any interviews on the days that they pitch. And, of course, George is the staunchest advocate of this rule.

But, as I said, I don't believe in it. The reporters got a job to do, too, and the better you get along with them, the happier the both of you will be. So when an old buddy of mine from Dallas called me earlier in the week and asked if I'd go on live on his TV sports report today, I said that I'd be happy to.

So after I'd been at the park for awhile, one of the guys workin' with my buddy came into the clubhouse and asked me to come outside 'cause they were ready to go on the air. But when I got out on the field, I found a second camera crew waitin' for me too. This one was from CBS and they were here to film an interview with me that Dan Rather was supposed to run in the next few weeks. Safety had already told me that they'd be in sometime this week, so when they asked me to go on with them also I said that I would as soon as I finished with my buddy.

Then out of nowhere Joe Safety appears and grabs me by the arm and pulls me over to the side.

"I don't think you want to do this today, do ya?" he asks me.

And I say to myself, "What the hell is wrong with him? Hell, he should be glad that I'm doin' this shit. I mean, that's his job, makin' sure that the media is takin' care of. Hell, he should thank me for tryin' to make it so easy for him."

Then he motions his head upwards to the booth on the upper rim of the stadium where George is peering out of the window.

"George doesn't like this shit," he says, "and I'd feel a whole hell of a lot better if you didn't do this today."

Beads of sweat were startin' to form on his forehead, and I was startin' to feel real bad for him.

"Hey, Joe," I said, "if this is such a big thing for ya and it means that much, I'll do whatever you feel is right. If you don't feel that I should do it today, I won't."

But overhearing me say this, the group from CBS started gettin' real nervous. Hell, they'd come all the way down here to talk to me and if they couldn't interview me today, they'd have to stay another day, another day in Texas!

So the head guy from CBS grabbed Joe by the arm and asked him very politely to please make an exception in his case. By that time the beads of perspiration on Joe's forehead had turned to buckets.

"Hey"—Joe, normally a mild-mannered guy, starts screamin' at the guy—"I told ya the guy is pitchin' today. I told ya that if ya wanna do it tomorrow, that he'll do it tomorrow. But the guy ain't gonna do it today."

I'm just standin' there listenin' to all this shit and feelin' like a real ass, 'cause I know that there's really no real reason that I can't do the son of a bitch. But then I feel real sorry for Joe, 'cause I know that if I do, the son of a gun may lose his job.

Finally, the guy from CBS more or less sensed what was really goin' on and decided to back off to make things a little easier for everybody.

"Well, I guess we got mixed up," he says to Joe very nicely.

But Joe is all riled up now, uncontrollable, in fact, and he starts screaming at the guy, fully aware that George is still watching from above. "We didn't get mixed up," Joe screams, "you just can't have the guy today, O.K.?"

Then Joe walked away, somewhat satisfied that another minor disaster, namely the loss of his job, had been averted. But this guy from CBS, who was a real prankster, just couldn't leave things alone. So he grabs his cameraman and sneaks up behind Safety and sticks his microphone in his face, as if he was interviewing him, and says, "Joe, would you please explain to the national television audience why you won't let Phil Niekro talk to me today?"

Joe just went wild. His arms started goin' every which way and his feet started carryin' him away from the guy just as fast as they could—screaming at the guy all the while. "If you want to do it, do it goddamnit! But don't call me. No, sir, don't call me."

Now, why would anybody ever say that it's difficult to work for George Steinbrenner?

I was put in the position today of havin' to put a stop to our five-game losing streak. But I got plenty of support. We're a real proud bunch. Adversity and embarrassment seem to inspire us.

We just jumped all over this rookie named Cook by scoring six runs off him in the first six innings and another eight the rest of the way.

I gave up only one run and five hits through seven, but Billy lifted me in favor of Allen. Billy just doesn't believe that I'm strong enough to go nine. Which kinda pisses me off. Allen allowed only three hits and a run over the last two innings, and we won 14–2. But I still wanted to talk to Billy about why he lifted me.

So after the game, he and I were havin' a few drinks in the hotel bar and he started talkin' about the game. Right then and there I was gonna ask him why he took me out, but he started talkin' about Allen instead.

"Hey, I know pitchin'. I know pitchin'," he kept sayin' over and over. "And I'm gonna turn that kid's whole life around. He's gonna be a great pitcher under me."

I didn't know what the hell to say to that, and I didn't want to get into one of his patented barroom brawls with him, so I just let it go.

I ran into George in the hotel elevator before today's game, and he made reference to the fact that he thought Billy left Guid in a little too long last night and that was why we lost the game.

"Good luck tonight," he said, "but don't do what Guidry did, goddamnit! If the heat starts gettin' to ya, you tell Billy to come out and get ya. Ya know, us old guys gotta take care of ourselves."

I just looked at him straight in the eye and kiddingly said, "I wouldn't know."

But I usually don't care if somebody kids me about my age. I guess it just depends on who's doin' the kiddin'. In fact, I guess I kinda see it as a compliment coming from some folks. Again, some folks that is!

But what does bother me is when people just keep askin' me the same damn question: "When ya gonna retire?" I don't know when I'm gonna retire and nobody can convince me why a forty-seven- or forty-eight-year-old man can't continue to play baseball. Someone has to be the oldest player in the game and I guess that I just have to be that person.

Another thing that pissed me off was when I lost five games in a row and people automatically started sayin' that I was over the hill, washed up. Bullshit! There're younger guys having far worse stretches than that, and nobody ever bothers them with any shit like that. But with me, two losses in a row means curtain time.

Too many people judge me on my age instead of my ability. How do you know you can't do somethin', no matter what your age, unless you try?

Toronto won again, so we're still six games out. Every game is gettin' bigger and bigger for us with the way they're playin'. Detroit lost again. So they're now tied for third place with the Red Sox, at eight and a half back.

Sunday, July 28 — TEXAS

When you're comin' back off a long stay on the D.L. like Marty Bystrom, you're really the only one who knows what you are capable of doin'. You're really the only one who knows how you feel and what you've got out there.

That's why it was ridiculous to have Marty's game called from the dugout today, pitch by pitch. All he really did was stand out there and throw the damn thing. No wonder he got his head beat in.

Oddibe McDowell hit his very first pitch of the season for a homer and the Rangers went on to score five runs in the first. Then they came back to score two more in the second, but Marty was already gone by that time. He only lasted one and two-thirds innings.

But it really wasn't all his fault 'cause they didn't allow him to throw any fastballs, which are his out pitches. All they'd let him throw were breaking balls. No wonder he got his ass kicked, and we ended up losing 8–2.

Billy started gettin' some real bad pains in his lower back about the second inning tonight and left the dugout to go back to the first-aid station. He was gone for four innings. You should have seen the look on the umps' faces when they saw him walking up the runway. It was almost like they'd just been given a vacation for the afternoon or somethin'.

When Billy returned to the dugout, he looked like he was in terrible pain. But he stuck around for the rest of the game before he let 'em take him to the hospital.

He was diagnosed as havin' a punctured lung. I guess the Rangers' team physician, who's an old friend of Billy's, gave him an injection to relax his back and ended up goin' a little too deep with the needle. Billy just has no luck.

Our loss today coupled with the Jays win not only dropped us seven games back, but also clinched the pennant for the Blue Jays, should the season conclude on the August 6 strike deadline. With that news, I bet that Billy felt like that needle had penetrated his heart instead of his lung.

Marty told me that Clyde King, who does the majority of George's work for him, called down after the game and asked him for his permission to send him down to Columbus.

I just can't believe it. A guy hasn't pitched in the big leagues for over eight months. In his first time back he throws the ball really well, but isn't allowed to throw his out pitch and ends up getting his brains beat out. So they call him a few hours later and give him the choice of either being sent down to Columbus or put back on the D.L.

That sucks. Marty didn't give Clyde an answer. He said he'd let him know tomorrow.

Monday, July 29 — CLEVELAND

My brother, Joe, called me this morning. With all this talk about me goin' back to Atlanta to manage, he wanted to know if I'd heard anything new. I told him that I hadn't, probably not any more than he'd heard.

But he also called to talk to me about his situation in Houston, where he was gonna be a free agent at the end of the year. Since his negotiations for a new contract had basically broken off, he wanted to know what was gonna happen to me, for his own benefit, too. 'Cause since it looked like he and the Astros weren't gonna be able to get together on anything, he thought that they'd try to trade him to a contender before the end of the season, a move that he could either accept or veto.

If he accepted it, he thought that he'd probably end up signing with the club they traded him to. If he vetoed any trades, he'd go free agent. That's why he called, to see if I thought I was gonna go back to Atlanta or not. If I thought I was gonna go back, then he'd veto any trades and see if he could go back with me.

But before he solidified any plans, he wanted to know if I thought that Ted had any interest in him. I told him that I didn't know, but that I would be happy to contact Ted for him.

I called Ted later that afternoon. I had to talk to him anyway, 'cause I wanted to see if he could arrange for me to wear a Braves uniform for the ceremonies that they were planning for me in Atlanta instead of a Yankees uniform. I just felt that it would be more appropriate.

We started out with some small talk, and I just asked him how he was doin'.

"Not so well," he told me, "everything down here is real messed up."

"I know," I replied. "I'm suffering right along with ya."

"Ya know," he told me, "the worst thing that I ever did was let you go."

I was really touched. In fact, tears started to well up in my eyes, so I switched the subject real quick to Joe, explained the situation and asked if he'd be interested. In his own way, but in a way to side-step any tampering allegations, he told me that he'd do anything he could to strengthen his ball club. I took that to mean yes.

There was only one other question that I wanted to ask him, about all that I'd been reading about in the papers. But I kinda felt that he'd answered that before I even got a chance to ask it. I just tried to hang up as quick as I could, just so I could dry my eyes and blow my nose.

George was quoted in a Cleveland paper today as saying that "Billy is managing as well as anyone has ever managed in any league anywhere." Sounds like the kiss of death to me.

I think Billy, who's paranoid about bein' fired anyway, thought so too 'cause he had tonight's lineup made up even before our plane landed in Cleveland and phoned it in to Lou Piniella, who was appointed as Billy's replacement, as soon as we arrived at the hotel.

Then at about fifteen minutes before game time, we got a call in the dugout. It was Billy. The Indians had arranged it so that he could talk directly to our dugout from his hospital bed.

Unfortunately for Butch, he was the one who answered the phone and Billy wanted to know everything that was goin' on. Who was battin'. Who was on deck. What the count was. Where the defense was playin'. What the last pitch was. Everything.

Butch just kept feedin' him all this information, kinda like doin' a question and answer play by play. There were a few of us sittin' down at the other end of the dugout with him, listenin' in. And we just thought that this whole thing was just as funny as hell. Then Butch started to look like he was gettin' real tired, like he was gonna need someone to take over for him, and we scattered like rats jumping off a sinking ship. The next thing I knew, all of us—players, trainers, equipment guys, everybody—were piled down into the far end of the dugout, like a band of passengers thrown together at the low end of a tossing ship, as far away from Butch and that damn phone as we could get.

Finally, Butch had to hang up on Billy just to catch his breath. And according to a Cleveland newspaper, when Billy called back a few minutes later, Peter Bavasi (the Indians' GM, who's a real card), had Billy's call sent over to the Indians' dugout, instead of ours, where I heard that Pat Corrales gave him a real earful.

Even with Billy only here in spirit, we won 8–2. But Toronto won too, so we're still seven out.

Tuesday, July 30 — CLEVELAND

With Billy still hooked up by phone, we split a doubleheader with the Indians. We won the first game 8–5, and Cowls won his ninth.

Cleveland had taken an early 3–1 lead, but we came back to score seven runs in the last three innings. Fish and Bordi combined to finish the last three innings and snuff out an Indian rally in the bottom of the ninth.

These Indians always play us tough. I guess that they just don't have much else to live for up here. Their fans come out to boo us more than cheer for the Tribe. In a city that's goin' as bad economically as Cleveland, our success and prestige as an organization breeds jealousy and envy. They come out to boo, not only the Yankees, but everything we represent. In Cleveland, we're not only a big draw, we're the only draw.

In the second game, the Indians unveiled a pair of no-names, a kid named Romero, who started, and another named Thompson, who pitches like Cleveland's version of Quisenberry. They stuck our bats up our asses and beat us 3–2.

The Jays lost to Baltimore, so we're now six and a half back.

Griff is still sufferin' through some pretty tough personal problems. In between games of the doubleheader, he went in and got dressed and was gonna leave until Lou talked him into stayin'.

Omar wants out real bad, too. He refused to play tonight. He says that he still has a bad back. Bullshit. He just wants to force George to trade him, which I'm sure George would just love to do, if he could find somebody that'd take him.

Mickey Hatcher of the Twins, who's a real crazy guy, has been sufferin' from a real bad back, an injury that I heard might even end his career.

Well, the other day he slipped in the shower and fell on his ass, and now his back is all better.

I heard that George is so pissed at the Count that he's considerin' tryin' the same therapy on him to help him with his hip. Only I heard that, instead of having him fall in a shower, that George is considerin' droppin' him from the roof of a twelve-story building. George always did like to do things in a big way.

Wednesday, July 31—CLEVELAND

Forster accepted Letterman's challenge and appeared on his show last night. Terry started out his act by walking on stage and handing Letterman a tongue sandwich. Then he proceeded to trade insults with Letterman for a few minutes before mixin' up a batch of his famous bullpen tacos to give to the audience.

He was a smash. I heard that he's even gonna be coming out with a new fitness video, á la Jane Fonda, entitled "Fat Is In."

Of all the teams to lose it to, Guid got his record of twelve consecutive decisions snapped tonight by the Cleveland Indians. With a streak as great as that you expect to lose it in a tough pitching match-up against a top-notch team. But the Cleveland Indians?

The Tribe wasn't even gracious or gentle about it. They just jumped all over his ass.

The loss dropped us to eight and a half games behind Toronto, who beat the Orioles again.

Thursday, August 1—CLEVELAND

We're playin' horseshit, and I'm no exception. I got my ass kicked royally by the Cleveland Indians today. Six runs in two and two-thirds innings. I was terrible.

While I was getting beat to death, this kid by the name of Roy Smith, who hadn't pitched since takin' a line drive off the forehead a few months ago, shut us down.

If Cleveland played us every day, not only would they draw a hell of a lot better, but they'd be in first place.

Ever since he was a kid, Ted has always wanted to own one of the major TV networks, and he came pretty close to getting CBS until the folks at CBS were somehow able to block his bid today. But all was not lost because Ted's attempted buy-out raised the price of CBS stock substantially. In fact, according to Dan Rather, Ted wound up making five million dollars on the CBS stock he already owned. I'll have to keep that in mind when I'm talkin' contract with him next year.

Friday, August 2—NEW YORK

Tonight was Polish-American Night at the Stadium. Jimmy Serr, my old buddy, and his polka band played before the game. They made me get up and dance a few numbers with some of the ladies they had all dressed up in their polka outfits. I wasn't too bad. But these unis just weren't made to polka in. But even as average as I was, my dancing still may have been the best play of the game. We're really goin' bad.

In the eighth inning tonight, with the game tied at 3–3 and with Meach at second, Yog at first and no outs, Hendy hit a gapper into left-center, and Yog pulled the boner of the year.

He ran into Meach at second, knocking him to one knee, then ran through Stick's sign at third and straight into a 8–6–2–2 double play at home—and on national TV. I just couldn't believe it and neither could NBC, who just kept running and rerunning the play, over and over again for the millions of viewers to giggle and gawk at.

While all this was happenin', I scrambled back inside to the clubhouse to call my dad, who I figured was watching the game. I just wanted to make sure that he was O.K. I just wasn't sure if his heart could take seein' something like that, especially replayed over and over again for four innings. But my mom had the good sense to turn off the TV after he'd seen it replayed about a half-dozen times.

Billy told the media after the game, "They got rid of the wrong Berra."

Saturday, August 3 — NEW YORK

When we all, including Billy, got to the ball park today, we learned that Mark Connor had been fired. Billy hadn't had anything to do with it. In fact, he hadn't even known anything about it and he was just as surprised as anyone. Hell, he thought that Mark was doin' a real fine job. But now he's gone, just another pawn in the game, the nineteenth pitching coach to be replaced by George since he took over the club. Now, that's a record even Finley couldn't beat.

Whit, who was our scheduled starter for today, was the most upset. He and Mark are real close. In fact, it was basically because of Mark that Whit had turned himself around. Mark had calmed Whit down, taught him how to handle the environment around here and restored his confidence.

Just before the game, Mark came around and shook all our hands and said good-bye. He's a real class act. His last stop was Whit's locker. By the time he got there, he had tears in his eyes. He just held out his hand for Whit to shake, and with a real determined look in his eye said, "Do it one time for me."

Whit answered immediately, "You got it."

And get it he did, not just from Whit but from all of us. We knew that Mark had gotten fired because of our horseshit play on national TV last night, and we all felt real bad. The least we could give him, we thought, was a goin' away present, which we did.

Whit wasn't at his best today, but he was tough, mentally tough, like Mark had taught him to be, and that's what pulled him through. He gave up twelve hits and four runs, but there was a fire in his eyes that I hadn't seen there before. He was gonna win this game no matter what.

As fired up as we all were about Mark's firing this morning and our embarrassing loss last night, we scored four runs in the first inning. Then we scored one more in the third, two in the fifth, and one in the sixth.

All in all on the day, we rapped out thirteen hits and three home runs, including Pasqua's two-run dinger in the first, which Hass followed with a solo shot, his sixth of the season. Though our 8–4 thumping of the Sox could never make up for the mockery of last night, at least we redeemed ourselves before a national TV audience today and showed the viewers that the Yankees are indeed a team to be reckoned with.

George hired Bill Monboquette to take Mark's place. He was at the park today with specific orders from George that his first role as our pitching coach was to work with Bordi on how to cover first base.

Bordi, Donny, and Yog were all fined severely for their parts in last night's loss. Rich and Donny were also told to be at the park early today to work on the play at first that they botched last night. Yog was just buried deeper and deeper in Billy's shithouse.

Sunday, August 4 — NEW YORK

Only 27,000 Pollocks showed up on Friday night to see me polka but 57,000 fans turned out today to see one of the classiest guys in the game, Tom Seaver, go after his three hundredth victory. Tom and I have been buddies for a long time and nobody was happier for him than me—and nobody was unhappier than George.

But it didn't start out that way. In fact, right before the game today, George had one of the kids from the promotion department come down and ask me if I would participate in a ceremony for Tom, if he did win No. 300 today, at the pitcher's mound right after the game. He wanted me to present Tom with a silver bowl from the Yankees to commemorate the event. I said, "Hell ya. I'd be happy to."

Tom wound up pitchin' a typical Tom Seaver game. Even though we took an early 1–0 lead, he was in command the whole way. Then in the sixth, Cowls and Fish got lit up for four runs and the crowd went berserk. From that time forward, there was just a constant chant goin' around the stadium: LEEETTT'SSS GOOOO MEEETTTSSS, LEEETTTTT'SSSS GOOOOO MEEEETTTSSSS!

It was exciting as hell. The crowd cheered on every pitch. I was just so intensely watchin' him that I actually felt I was out there with him, like the beating of my heart was actually his.

Flowing on the momentum of both the crowd and the moment, Tom just seemed to keep getting stronger. He mowed down our guys like they weren't even there.

Then after Baylor hit a fly ball to left to end the game, the place went bananas. The fans were cheering at the top of their lungs, Tom was jumpin' all over the place, and I felt like goin' out there and huggin' him myself.

Caught up in the whole emotion of the thing, I was real excited to get on with the ceremony. I just wanted to share both with Tom and the fans exactly how I felt. But as I stood around watching all the merriment, I noticed that no preparations were being made to ready the field for the presentation. No microphones, no nothin'. Then the same kid that George had sent down to ask me to present Tom with the bowl showed up.

"*Um, ah*, Phil, I mean *ah*, Mr. Niekro, there's been a change of plans. *Ah*, Mr., *ah*, Mr. Steinbrenner thinks that the, *um*, fans will storm down onto the field if we do somethin' like this. So he wants you to present the bowl to Seaver in the dugout."

In the dugout? For who . . . the batboys? Bullshit! That's bullshit! There were enough security guys surrounding the field to wrestle King Kong to the ground. George was just ticked off because of all the Mets fans who were here. But that was still no reason to take it out on Tom.

I finally just said to myself, "Screw it," and tried to do the best that I could. I just waited until Tom left the White Sox dugout and headed across the field, over toward our dugout, to do an interview with one of the network guys who was waitin' for him.

Then I ran out onto the field, where I hoped that at least a few fans would see the presentation, and grabbed Tom by the arm.

He was still up. Hell, he was a million miles away and I could just feel the happiness running out of him. What a setting for a presentation like this. But he was so happy that he didn't seem to care.

"Congratulations, Tom," I said as I handed him the bowl. "This is from the entire Yankee organization. Again, congratulations. You were great."

Caught up in all that was goin' on, he just patted me on the back, thanked me, and said, "You're next buddy."

I walked back into the clubhouse kinda dejected because of the horseshit way I was made to go about the presentation. When I got to my locker, which is within earshot of Billy's office, I could hear George screamin' at the top of his lungs.

"Let's go Mets, Let's go Mets! What the fuck, Billy? Your guys didn't even look like they were tryin' out there? And why, Billy, why, does it always fuckin' happen here?

"Perry and fuckin' Seaver! Perry and fuckin' Seaver, Billy! I hate to be the fuckin' answer to some fuckin' trivia question! Why'd you have to let the son of a bitch win it here? Why couldn't he have won it in some other fuckin' place? Why does it always have to fuckin' happen here at Yankee Stadium?

"Can't you get those fuckin' guys to hit, Billy? What the fuck? What the fuck, Billy? Let's Go Mets, Let's Go Mets! What the fuck, Billy? What the . . ."

I guess that not everybody was happy for Tom.

Lost in all the celebration was the fact that Rod Carew got his three thousandth hit today. Some fans have been critical of Carew 'cause they say that he can't hit in clutch situations. Shit, they've never had to pitch against him.

According to Ira Berkow of the *Times*, Carew hit .389 over his career in clutch situations. Whoever says that shit about Carew has either never played against him or hasn't followed his career very closely.

The Commissioner was on both "Face the Nation" and David Brinkley's show today to talk about the possibility of an upcoming strike. According to Ubie, "There will be no strike." I just hope he's right 'cause that's the last thing I want. Hell, at my age, you need all the days you can get.

But I think that if anybody can stop this thing from gettin' out of hand, it'll be him. He's got a lot of balls, and he's a real straight shooter.

But Ubie will probably get some opposition from a few of the clubs who are probably in favor of a strike, like San Francisco and Pittsburgh. In those towns, where the seagulls and pigeons at the ball park outnumber the fans, they'd actually make out better financially if their teams didn't play.

With their team doin' so poorly, I guess that about the only thing those fans in Pittsburgh are gonna miss are those great cow-milking contests. Yeah, those have always been one of my favorites, too.

George is really worryin' about discipline around here. So he's been discussin' with Billy about having more rules for the players. Billy listens to him, even though he doesn't agree with him.

The other day, George said that not enough of the players were in the dugout during the game, so he instituted a rule that no players were allowed in the clubhouse during a game, no matter what.

Yog was caught in the clubhouse today. It cost him $250. Funny thing was that he could have stayed in there for a whole month of games a few days ago and nobody would have missed him. But now he's fined $250 for not bein' around. But either way, he's not gonna play again around here.

Monday, August 5 — NEW YORK

I'm not in favor of this strike shit at all, but then I don't think anybody else is either. We don't even know what all the issues really are. Like me, most guys just want to play ball.

I don't need a raise and neither do the majority of the guys that play this game. If you're gonna give somebody a raise, give it to the president. Most of us make more money than he does anyway, and all we gotta do is go out and play ball. Daily, he's gotta do battle with guys with names like Brezhnev and Khomeini. You talk about being underpaid, that's the president. He's the one that should go on strike. Not us!

It was real confusin' around here today. Nobody seemed to know what was goin' on. Baylor told us to get our things packed and to take 'em with us after the game, but to stay close just in case they settled this thing early enough to play tomorrow's game.

What a sorry sight. Nobody really wanted to go out on strike. In fact, I think that if they were to present all the issues clearly to us today and take another vote that there would be no strike. But then that's probably why they took the vote so early, before our minds got involved emotionally.

But none of us wanna go. Hell, we may be nine games out, but we're still in the pennant race. And we're havin' fun. Even guys like Don Mattingly don't want to go out on strike. And Donny could go to arbitration this year and probably walk away with a whole ton of bucks. A new time limit on arbitration is one of the things they're presently arguing about. But Donny doesn't really care. He just wants to play, and so do the rest of us.

Guid was about the only one who didn't seem real confused. He went out there tonight and was just his usual self, as he won his fourteenth. But I've never seen the clubhouse this down after a win. Most of the guys just got their shit together and left, not knowing whether we would end up in a tie for second place with Detroit at nine back, or if we'd get another shot at catching Toronto.

But one thing is in our favor. The Mets moved into first place today. Which means that if the season ended today, they'd win the pennant, and there's no way that George'll stand for that. Look for him to get involved in this strike stuff and for this son of a gun to be settled real quick. The Mets finishing in first and the Yanks in second, that'd be un-American!

There are a lotta casualties in a strike. Both sides get hurt. But I don't think there could be a bigger casualty than Mike Armstrong, who was recalled today, just so the club wouldn't have to pay him during the strike and so Pasqua could go back to Columbus and keep in shape during the strike.

Poor Army, just when he was starting to get his shit back together too. He may never recover from this one.

Wednesday, August 7—ATLANTA

I was happy to get home for a few days, but I was even happier when the strike ended. At my age, you don't know how many more pennant races your career is gonna hold for you.

I actually wasn't gonna come home at all, but then Nancy called yesterday and reminded me that I had forgot our anniversary. I just said to myself, "shit," and got on the first plane home this morning.

Nancy is that one constant factor in my life that never changes. She's always wanting the best for me and she's always there whether I'm in the middle of a losing streak or have been released. She's that one aspect of my life that never sways or changes. And the love that I have for her will never change.

After I got home, I chased her around the house a few times. We talked and laughed like always. It was good to be home. But then the phone rang. The strike was over and it was back to the pennant race as fast as my little feet could carry me.

Thursday, August 8—NEW YORK

George and Billy really screwed up by recalling Army, 'cause now they're stuck with him for at least ten days before they can recall Pasqua. And there's no way that they're gonna use him. So what do they plan to do with him?

Poor Army, he's just another useless body on this ball club, and he was just startin' to get his confidence back too. I even heard that he smiled once in Columbus. But now, he's back to his old ways. Today, I saw him run into the outfield fence three times shagging balls. Each one looked like a suicide attempt to me.

. . .

Everybody was back in time for today's doubleheader except for Hendy. Hell, I flew outta Atlanta this morning and was back here by this afternoon. Fish was all the way out in Colorado and busted his ass to get back here today, in time for the doubleheader.

But Hendy flew outta here to California late yesterday afternoon after the agreement had already been reached. He knew an agreement had been reached, too, 'cause Winnie talked to him that afternoon and told him so. But he still left anyway.

That was totally uncalled for. We're in a pennant race! We're nine games out, but we're still in a pennant race! Damn, we need to win every game we can to catch Toronto and him doin' shit like this is not gonna help us at all.

But even without Hendy, we still looked great tonight. Willie filled in for Rickey in the leadoff spot. He came up with three hits and scored three runs in the first game. Winnie, who's really taken over the reins as our emotional leader, went three for three, with two dingers, and drove in six runs. And Billy Sample, who started in center for Hendy, went three for four.

Marty started the first game but struggled and was gone after the fifth. Then Billy brought in Fish, Shirls, and Allen, who combined for four innings of hitless relief.

In the second game, I started and got my Polish sausage kicked in. I think it was all that chasing around of Nancy yesterday. I usually run in between starts, but never that much.

So Billy had to go to the bullpen early again. Fish came in and pitched another two and two-thirds. Rags finished up, and we held on to win 7–6 and sweep the doubleheader. Unfortunately, the Jays also swept a doubleheader, so we didn't pick up any ground on them. But Detroit got swept by the Royals, who are really playin' well. It's gettin' more and more obvious that to win this thing we're gonna have to win every game possible, 'cause I don't think we can count on Toronto folding.

Sparky Anderson is still really ticked off at Billy for what Billy said about his handling of Hendy at the All Star Game. Sparky was quoted in the paper today as trying to make jest of the fact that everybody thinks that George tells Billy who to play each night, namely the highest-paid players.

"I'd quit in a minute," he said today in the newspaper, of Billy's supposed position. "I wasn't hired to be the team's accountant." No shit, Sparky! You're real fuckin' lousy with numbers. When was the last time you checked the standings and saw by how many games you trailed both us and Toronto?

Friday, August 9 — BOSTON

Hendy was back in town today, but his wallet was $22,000 lighter. George really got his ass for not being here to restart the season. This is the first time since I've been here that I've agreed with a player being fined. Hendy could have cost a pennant by not being here yesterday. Thank God we still swept the Indians without him. But if we had lost either one of those games on a situation where he could have won it for us, I think George would have fined him maybe ten times as much, a move I would have definitely applauded.

But all seemed cleared up tonight, 'cause Hendy was again his old self on the diamond. One thing about Hendy, even though he does screw up occasionally, he is a real smart kid.

Tonight, he was once again the key man in our attack and was responsible for starting our six-run rally in the sixth that eventually led to our 10–6 win.

But Billy had to go deep into our bullpen again, 'cause Whit lasted only four innings. Bordi, Shirls, and Rags had to take over from that point—and held the Sox to only two hits over the last five innings. How much longer Billy's gonna be able to keep dippin' into the bullpen, though, I don't know. You never know, Army may just become a real valuable asset around here.

The Jays lost to the Royals, who are really playin' good ball. So we finally picked up a game on 'em. Those guys are tough though. Every game is crucial at this point. We're gonna have to win a hell of a lot more than they do from this point forward, if we want to walk away with the pennant. Well, then, on second thought, maybe Army won't get in.

Saturday, August 10 — BOSTON

The best part about playin' on a pennant contender is after the game, when you walk into the clubhouse and see twenty-five guys havin' a good time. I mean, really livin', laughin', smilin', playin' pranks on each other. It's great.

It's no fun if you go out and pitch a one- or two-hitter, then wind up getting beat 1–0. It's like a morgue. Everybody's head is down and they just walk around second-guessing themselves.

But when you're in a pennant race, there's nothing better. Individual stats don't mean shit. All you really care about is winning. You lust for it, it's fun, and it becomes all that matters. You don't even think about who screwed up, or if you screwed up. All's nullified by winning.

In one game this season, Pasqua struck out three outta four at-bats but then made a great catch in the late innings to save the game, and we wound up winning. That play looked as big as any three-run homer he could've hit.

When you're winning, plays like that are what you remember. You remember only the good things, the catches, the key hits, the important strikeouts. You focus only on the good and your confidence skyrockets as a result. That's what makes being in one of these suckers so thrilling. And that's how all of us are feelin' right now.

In April, Oil Can Boyd stuck our bats up our asses. He intimidated us with his fastball by buzzin' our big guys. But we're a different team now, a team with a reason, one brimming with confidence, and we kicked his cocky ass good tonight. It felt great. We all laughed about it in the clubhouse after the game.

But the best thing about tonight was that our win moved us another game closer to Toronto, who lost again to the red-hot Royals.

Unfortunately, Billy isn't gonna be around with us for a while. The lung he punctured started acting up again, and he had to be taken to the hospital after the game.

Shit like this just never seems to stop around here. There are rumors that he might not rejoin us for the rest of the season, which would be a real shame. He's been such an active force in getting us to where we're presently at. And this kinda excitement is what Billy was made for. I just can't see him missin' too many games though. Hell, I think he'd lay down his life to be a part of another pennant race.

George has used the occasion of Billy's illness to stir up some shit. He seems to love to do that. Already he's got the media buzzin' about whether or not Billy'll be back or not. He's also appointed Lou Piniella as Billy's replacement, which has also stirred up a lotta dirt, 'cause the media has been building Lou up as Billy's replacement should he get fired. George has got them all askin' themselves whether Billy will ever manage another game for the Yankees. He's good at stirring up that shit.

A reporter walked over to Shirls today and started makin' small talk and asked Shirls what he did during the strike. Shirls, who's a real funny guy, just got this weird look on his face and started tellin' the guy about how he took his family on a very disappointing ride on the Staten Island Ferry.

"My middle kid was hysterical," Shirls said. "He was afraid of the boat. Plus, he thought there were sharks out there. We didn't see any sharks though. Some dead bodies, but no sharks."

I heard that George is gonna be going on Letterman's show in the next few weeks. Let's see. Letterman had Forster make tacos and me throw my knuckler. I wonder what George is gonna do? Fine somebody? You're guess is as good as mine.

Sunday, August 11—BOSTON

I'd much rather sweep a series in August than in April. I think that's kinda how everyone around here feels about it. The Red Sox demoralized us at the beginning of the season, but now we're back here kickin' their ass when it really counts.

Guid was our big guy today. He made it into the seventh before Billy, who rose from his death bed to be with us today, brought in Shirls and then Fish to close the game out.

The win was our sixth in a row and kept us at seven games back of the Jays, who finally beat the Royals.

Hass has been just phenomenal for us this season. I think that when the Yanks got him from the Cubs, the best they were hopin' for was a left-handed hitting back-up catcher who could play about once a week. But with Hass they got a whole hell of a lot more.

With Butch bein' hurt so much, Hass has been more than just a fill-in; he's been an inspiration. He's havin' the finest year of his career. He just always seems to come up with the big hit or big play whenever we need it.

Hass came down with a stomach virus today and all of us are really concerned. 'Cause word around here has it that George is gonna activate Dom.

Monday, August 12 — CHICAGO

Hass, fresh from his sickbed, hit two dingers tonight, for the second time this season, and staged a seven-run seventh that really saved my ass. I was really draggin' going into the sixth. But that seven-run seventh gave me the momentum I needed to finish the game—and gave our bullpen a much needed day of rest.

Hell, the bullpen has been carrying our asses over the entire length of this winning streak. In fact, they're the prime reason that this streak has reached seven games. When we get an early lead, they hold it. When we fall behind early, they come in and hold the other guys until we get a chance to catch up.

But if it hadn't been for their needed rest and our large lead, there's no way that Billy would have let me finish this one, no matter how well I pitched. He just doesn't think that I have it in me anymore.

Our win brought us to within six of Toronto, who lost to those fightin' Texas Rangers.

Tuesday, August 13 — CHICAGO

Marty seems to be really gettin' his shit together. He had a no-hitter goin' through four and two-thirds, and a one-hitter goin' through six and a third. Unfortunately, the Sox came back to win it. The bullpen just couldn't hold 'em this time. I just can't remember the last time that the bullpen didn't hold a game for us.

Fish got the loss, and Ozzie Guillen, who's really played well against us, scored the winning run on a sacrifice fly to beat us. The loss dropped us back to seven games behind the Jays.

Ever since his appearance on Letterman's show, Forster has made heroes of fat people everywhere. As I mentioned before, he's even gonna be comin' out with a video called "Fat Is In." Which got me to thinkin', why couldn't I come out with my own video and call it "It's Fun To Be Old," where I would simply sit in front of a camera for thirty minutes and laugh my ass off.

Billy came out of his office after the game and called us all over. He looked terrible. I thought that he was gonna tell us that the punctured lung that he had was contagious or somethin'. But the news was even worse than that: Pete Sheehy, our legendary clubhouse guy, had died.

Wednesday, August 14 — CHICAGO

Pete left a part of himself behind with all of us, more than I think even he thought he would. Not so much in the name that hangs over our clubhouse or in the memories some of the guys have of him, but instead in the pride that he helped instill in all our minds, especially Billy's.

I guess Pete was like a father to Billy. And when he died, a certain part of Billy died with him, but a certain aspect of Billy also came back to life, a side which Billy had compromised to get his job with the Yankees back, the fightin' don't-take-any-shit-from-anybody, even George, attitude that has made him into the manager that he is.

Though we had seen signs of it all season long, we never really felt it to the degree that we have since Pete died. Today Billy threw all those damn compromises he had to make out the window and overruled George by canceling an off-day workout that George had scheduled for us tomorrow at the stadium. Which may not seem like a big step, but it was.

George was just kinda taken aback by the whole thing. He's just so used to always getting his own way. But he didn't challenge Billy's actions. In fact, he went on the defensive.

We all had respect for Billy before this incident, but we really respect him now. We all feel that he knows exactly what needs to be done to win the pennant and he's gonna do what he has to do, no matter what the costs. Even though Pete is now gone, the spirit of the Yankees is still alive, in Billy and thus in all of us.

Whit started and got blasted again. He's really gone downhill since Mark got fired. I think that when he told Mark that he'd "do it for him one more time," he must've taken himself literally, because he hasn't had a good outing since.

Tonight, he lasted only three innings and gave up five runs. But because of our bats, we were lucky to be behind by only two when he left. Then Billy brought in Shirls, a guy that just gets no respect around here.

Baylor once said, "To win a pennant, you gotta have guys like Bob Shirley on your club. But I don't know why."

Shirls came in tonight for Whit and pitched four scoreless innings. But Shirls didn't receive any official type of credit for his efforts, no save, no win. Only another funny smile from Billy.

But because of Shirl's efforts, we were able to fight our way back into the game, a game which we finally won when Hass, another guy who gets no respect, hit a two-run single in the ninth that won the game for us and kept us within seven of the Jays.

Thursday, August 15, OFF DAY—NEW YORK

We didn't get in from Chicago until real late, so I slept in. Then I decided to go out and make the best use of this off-day that Billy fought so hard to get for us. So after wakin' up in mid-afternoon, I went out and got shit-faced.

Friday, August 16 — NEW YORK

What a momentous day for George. First, we went out and beat the Red Sox, who he loves to hate almost as much as the Mets, and we did so by kickin' ol' Oil Can's ass again.

Then the Mets lost and fell out of first place. We beat Boston and the Mets fall out of first! Could George be any happier?

Kansas City beat the Jays again, so we've moved another game closer. We're now only six back. I tell ya, by the way they're playin' against Toronto, I think our MVP award should go to the Royals. Hell, they're the only team that can beat those guys.

After having tried to trade him away, or should I say give him away, George finally released Omar today to make room for Pasqua. Which means that Army's prison sentence has been extended. It also means that the clubhouse is gonna be a hell of a lot quieter with Omar gone.

There was an article in the newspaper about this Scottish golfer who was banned from the sport for the next twenty years for cheating. There are some of us around here who think that he's gonna be our next manager. He already has the win-at-any-cost attitude that George admires so much.

Saturday, August 17 — NEW YORK

With all the publicity surrounding Pete Rose's pursuit of Ty Cobb's record, there seems to be a quote by Pete in the paper almost every day. Today, there was a quote by him in the paper in which he talks about divorce. "Just give her a million bucks and tell her to hit the road," he said, very clear, very crisp, very concise, and very easy.

Strangely, though, that's the same exact philosophy that this club has about once-great Panamanian center-fielders named Moreno.

Those Royals did it again. They beat the Jays. Coupled with our win, Guid's sixteenth, we're now only five out.

Sunday, August 18 — NEW YORK

There's almost nothin' that New Yorkers love more than baseball. And there's nothin' that excites them more than the possibility of a subway series between us and the Mets, which is startin' to look like a real possibility, with the way we're both playin'.

Because of their intense love of the game, New Yorkers will do almost anything to see us or the Mets play, includin' riskin' their lives by ridin' the subways.

In fact, it was noted in the newspaper today that fans are takin' to the subways in record numbers to come to the games. And, of course, the Transit Authority is just happy as hell about that. As a result, I'm sure that the muggings are up by an equal amount. Isn't it just wonderful what a winning ball club can do for a city's economy?

I was worthless today, but we still won. I guess that shows ya just how good we're goin'.

But that ol' Yankee spirit carried us through today as we came back to take the lead in the seventh and Rags and Fish held 'em the rest of the way. The win kept us within five of the Jays, who finally beat K.C.

Monday, August 19 — NEW YORK

We completed our sweep of the Bosox today, but it didn't come easy. In fact, it took some key hits and two remarkable plays, one by Griff and the other by Shirls.

Though we had taken an early lead, the Sox quickly caught back up and rocked rockin' Marty pretty good. In fact, they had a 5–3 lead goin' into the seventh, when Winnie and Baylor knocked in three runs to put us back ahead.

But the Sox came storming back again in the ninth. That's when Shirls served up a fat one to Marty Barrett, the Sox's weak-hitting second baseman, who muscled the sucker into the left-field corner. It looked for sure like a home run. But Griff, as he seems to have done ten times already this year, drifted back into the corner, jumped, his glove stretching well into the confines of the charity section, and caught the son of a bitch.

It was one of the greatest catches I'd ever seen, and it won the game for us. But what did Shirls do that was so great? What role did he play that was so outstandin'? Well, as he says, "Someone had to throw that ball to Barrett. Right?"

Like Baylor said, "You need a guy like Bob Shirley on your club to win a pennant. But I don't know why."

You think that George would be happy just because of the way we're playin'. But that doesn't seem to be the case. I guess that pressure affects everybody differently, especially pennant pressure, and especially George.

Instead of goin' out and enjoyin' all this, like us, George went out and got Yog tested for drugs.

Though what George did may be against what the Players' Union has set up with the owners, and though all this may sound real fuckin' ridiculous, I do believe that George actually had Yog's best interests in mind when he did it. But at least all the stuff that George's actions will stir up will keep him busy for awhile.

The Cleveland Indians have lived in baseball's low-rent district for so long that the only thing they really look forward to each season is playin' the role of the spoiler. Which, probably because of their depth of experience, they probably do better than anyone in the big leagues.

Tonight, they beat the Jays and their best pitcher, Dave Stieb. Toronto's lead is now only four games. In fifteen days, we've won eleven out of twelve games and picked up five and a half games on Toronto.

Army, the twenty-seventh man on our twenty-six-man roster, was sent back to Columbus. He was with us a total of fourteen days. Over that time, he didn't appear in any games, didn't notch any wins, saves, or strikeouts. But he did run into the outfield fence one hundred and twelve times.

Tuesday, August 20 — CALIFORNIA

We gave Whit a 7–0 lead going into the fifth, but he couldn't hold it. In fact, he gave up four runs in that inning and wasn't even around when the decision was given out. Another day of overtime for the guys from the bullpen, who responded valiantly, as usual, holding the Angels to only one run over the next five innings.

We gotta get these guys from the bullpen some help. Right now, they're really draggin'. Guid and sometimes I are the only ones who consistently get into the seventh inning. We need some more starters. We need to give our bullpen a break. We could use somebody like my brother Joe.

Hell, George could probably get him from the Astros for a few minor leaguers. Joe's not gonna sign with the Astros anyway, so why shouldn't they try to unload him for whatever they can get? But the key is that we need him now. If George waits too much longer, it'll be too late and we won't be able to get him on the playoff roster anyway.

Shit, tonight Billy had to use three relievers to get the job done. But we did win 8–5, which was our sixth straight win since Billy stood up to George, a move that could carry this club emotionally for weeks.

Donny hit two homers tonight and drove in his one hundredth run. The kid is just phenomenal.

Hass was rushed to the hospital the other night, before we left on this roadtrip. He was in severe pain. He had to have a kidney stone removed, and he's gonna miss a few games.

If our catchers keep fallin' like this, it's only a matter of time before we don't have anyone left in the organization to call up but—you guessed it—Dom. I wonder if it's too late to get his name on the All Star ballot for next year?

The Cubs released Larry Bowa the other day and the Mets picked him up. Bowa, who's thirty-nine, said that he was lucky just to be playin' at his age. Then what the hell does that make me?

Wednesday, August 21—CALIFORNIA

What a game. One of the worst I've ever seen played, but amazingly we won.

Together with the Angels, we committed eight errors and scored nine unearned runs. We also used five pitchers. Cowls, who started, just couldn't get anybody out, not even one guy.

Tonight would have been a perfect night for Army. Even he would've gotten in. But then even Walter Johnson would have gotten in, even at his age, if he were alive and here.

Fittingly, we scored three runs in the top of the tenth, all unearned of course, to win it. Causing Billy to remark, "I guess you could call this one a laugher."

The red-hot Indians did it again, as they beat Toronto. We're now only three back.

Thursday, August 22—CALIFORNIA

We finally lost and strangely it came with Guid on the mound. But he didn't get the loss, Bordi did. Guid pitched eight strong innings but we just weren't able to get him any runs and we went into the ninth tied 2–2. Then Rich, who'd taken over by that time, walked Bobby Grich. Rags then came on to relieve him and Grich was sacrificed to second. Rags struck out the next guy; then Bob Boone, who was sufferin' from a pulled groin muscle, hobbled into the batter's box and stroked a single to left, scoring Grich. We would have actually had a better chance of throwing Boone out at first than Grich out at home. Hell, I could've ran backwards and kept up with him.

The loss dropped us another half-game behind Toronto, who didn't play today. Right now, it looks like it's only us and them to fight for the divisional pennant, 'cause Detroit is still holding at nine back.

Almost all George's time at the present moment is spent with the Player's Association over his decision to test Yog for drugs. Today, George sent them a 557 word statement describing in vivid detail the inadequacies of their present drug-detection system.

Whether he's right or wrong, whether the suggestions he made to them are good or bad, it doesn't really matter as long as it keeps him busy.

Rickey was supposedly evicted from his luxury condo the other day and the press around here picked up on it right away. One thing that the media is extremely good at is finding a guy's Achilles' heel and then snapping it. By doin' so, they sell a hell of a lot of newspapers.

Look what they've done to Billy. Hell, every major boxing promoter wants him—The Great Rematch: Billy versus the Marshmallow Salesman.

In Rickey's case, he's subletting from a guy who says that he owes him a few thousand in phone charges, back rent, garage charges, and shit like that. Rickey's landlord just better hope that George is tied with the Player's Association for awhile also. 'Cause if George runs out of things to fuck with and he hears about all this shit that Rickey has been takin', George may just turn all his energies in the direction of Hendy's landlord. I wouldn't wish that on anyone.

Ted just announced that Eddie Haas was his manager for the remainder of the season. Sounds like the kiss of death to me. He's fuckin' gone. Ted's just lookin' for a reason, another losin' streak or somethin', to run out of patience so he can fire him.

Eddie's a hell of a guy and a great teacher, but he seems to lack a few necessary ingredients that all big league managers have to have. Mainly, he doesn't bitch enough. Hell, I've heard that he's only been on the field, either arguing with an ump or defending one of his players, five times this year. Shit, Billy's on that field that many times even before the game begins, and he keeps fightin' all the way into the next mornin'.

Friday, August 23 — SEATTLE

No. 296 came pretty easy. The win was my twelfth of the season and my fifth in my last six decisions. As much as I've been able to keep from worrying about gettin' No. 300, I must admit that I'm actually consumed by the whole thing.

At first, I think that I subconsciously wanted to win it in Atlanta and only Atlanta, 'cause I felt that I owed it to the fans down there. But as this season progressed, I grew to believe that I was meant to win it this season, here in New York and in the middle of this pennant race. Could there be a better time or a better team to win it with? Hell no. As far as I am concerned, this is the perfect time and the perfect team with which to accomplish such a feat.

As the time grows nearer, I just can't wait for my next start. I'm presently living through what every kid that ever played the game dreamed of, at one time or another. This is what I've geared my life toward. That's why No. 300 has to come here, in the middle of all this, and during this, possibly my most memorable and exciting season.

I went six innings tonight and gave up only one run before my lower back stiffened on me, an old polka injury, and Billy brought Allen in to relieve me.

Billy is just inflamed with makin' Allen into the reliever he thinks he can be. Allen's main problem at this point is his confidence. He just has no confidence at all, no confidence in his fastball, no confidence in his curve, no confidence in himself.

But Billy's been workin' with him, and he's gettin' better. Billy brought him in tonight, and he basically shut everything down. I think just the fact that Billy gave him a chance to pitch in a close game boosted his confidence.

Though we won, we still dropped a half-game in the standings because the Jays swept a doubleheader from the White Sox. I just wish that they played the Royals and Indians every day. If they did, we'd be ten games in front.

The final game of the Little League World Series is tomorrow, between a team from Seoul, South Korea, and one from Mexicali, Mexico. As far as I'm concerned, the whole thing sounds kind of un-American to me.

Saturday, August 24 — SEATTLE

Tonight's game was Billy's kinda game. We got only two hits but wound up winning 4–3, by taking advantage of every walk they gave us and every miscue they made.

Though he gave up three runs in six innings, Marty started and pitched reasonably well. Then Billy, who's managin' like it was the seventh game of the World Series, started bringin' in his parade of relievers, one for almost every situation, four in all.

But every time he'd walk out to the mound, this drunken fool behind the dugout would give him an earful of shit. Finally, Billy, who's not one to turn down the opportunity to make a fool out of a fool, turned around and yelled at the guy, "How smart are you? You paid to see me! That's like payin' ten bucks to go to the zoo and then callin' the gorilla stupid."

The Jays won again. We're still four back.

Sunday, August 25 — SEATTLE

Whit lasted six and a third today and got the win, but the majority of the credit should go to the hitters, who made up for last night's effort by goin' out and scoring eight runs today.

Pasqua went three for four with a three-run homer and a double. Mattingly added a two-run homer and Hendy went three for four. The win was Whit's eighth. Billy brought in Allen again, but he looked terrible. So Fish had to finish up for him.

The White Sox finally beat the Jays, so we're now only three back.

Mom decided to call me all the way out here today. She's really upset because she still hasn't gotten her hats from George. She told me that she'd already bought the plane ticket for her and her umbrella and that she's coming to New York to see George.

I talked her out of it though. George can handle high-powered sports agents, the players' union, and shit like that, but I don't think he can handle my mom.

Monday, August 26 — OAKLAND

Eddie Haas was fired today and Bobby Wine was named to replace him for the remainder of the season. Ted hasn't called to talk to me about the position. But from what I've been hearin' and from what I got out of my conversation with him last month, I think I'm being seriously considered for the job.

At least I think that Ted'll give me a call either way before he makes a decision on who's gonna run the club next year. In fact, a few years ago, when he and I were out fishin' one day, we were discussin' the club and he told me that I'd be managin' the Braves one day. And Ted's a man of his word.

We lost tonight in fifteen innings, when former Yankee Dave Collins hit a two-out infield single to score the winning run. Those ex-Yankees just love to come back and give us the old red ass. And no team has more ex-Yankees than the A's. Hell, they've got half our team out here. But we got Hendy in the deal, so I guess you could say that we got our money's worth.

Our loss dropped us to four behind Toronto.

Tuesday, August 27 — OAKLAND

Tommy John beat us tonight by tossing a three-hitter. Tommy's pitchin' real good but he's also had his troubles, most of which were dealin' with his age. People around baseball circles just don't believe that you can play after a certain age and they are always looking for reasons to substantiate their beliefs.

That's what happened to me in Atlanta and that's what has been happening to Tommy over the last few years. Our age got us released, not our lack of ability.

So even though I was definitely pulling for us tonight, if we had to get beat I'm glad that it was by an old guy like Tommy. The baseball world is stacked against us, and we need all the help we can get.

. . .

Tommy beat Guid tonight. It was only Guid's fifth loss of the season. Mattingly and Baylor were the only guys to get any hits tonight. Tommy was really hittin' his spots.

Our loss dropped us to five games behind the Jays, who beat the Twins again. Where the hell are the Cleveland Indians when ya need 'em?

Bobby Wine is already 2–0 as the Braves' manager. Shit, if things keep goin' as they are, he may never lose. And not even George could replace an undefeated manager. Well, on second thought, maybe George could, but Ted wouldn't.

Wednesday, August 28, OFF DAY—NEW YORK

The Braves won again. They're now 3–0 under Wine, with only thirty-seven more games to go.

Thursday, August 29—NEW YORK

I've been doin' a lot of scoreboard watchin' lately. In fact, I haven't been able to take my eye off the scoreboard since Wine took over in Atlanta.

The Braves won again. They're now 4–0.

If I pitched against the California Angels every day, I would have had 300 wins ten years ago. I just don't know what it is, but I seem to always pitch well against them. Tonight I shut 'em out again. I've now gone somethin' like twenty-two or twenty-three innings against 'em without allowing a run.

But even with my 4–0 lead, Billy still yanked me out in the seventh and brought in Rags to finish up. As much as anybody, I think Billy is guilty of falling prey to this age shit. I could have easily finished tonight. Hell, these guys haven't hit me all season.

The win was the two hundred and ninety-seventh of my career. But the best part of tonight's experience was the fact that it brought us a half-game closer to Toronto, who didn't play today.

Friday, August 30 — NEW YORK

California kicked our ass today. John Candelaria, who the Angels got from Pittsburgh a few months ago, a guy that I heard we could've got, a guy we could truly use, pitched two-hit, shutout ball for five and a third, before Gene Mauch turned the game over to his reliable bullpen. We didn't even score a run until the seventh and wound up losing 4–1.

Marty started for us, looked bad and ended up hurting his elbow. As if we didn't have enough problems with our starters already. Shirls came in and shut 'em down for the last five, but we couldn't get him any runs.

I wish that the club would just go out and get us another starter, someone like Joe. Right now, Guid and I are the only two starters doin' diddley-squat around here and you can't win a pennant with only two reliable starters.

Atlanta won again. That's now five wins in a row for them, their longest winning streak of the season. I start sending out résumés to other clubs tomorrow.

Toronto also won again. We're now five back.

Saturday, August 31 — NEW YORK

Besides his confidence, Allen needs to be able to throw strikes with his curveball to be effective. That way, the hitters won't be able to sit back and wait on his fastball.

Today, Whit lasted only four and two-thirds, so Billy had to go to the bullpen early once again. Since we had a lead, he brought in Rags in the fifth to cool down the Angels, which he did. Then in the later innings, with us leading 10–4, Billy brought in Allen, featuring a wicked curveball. He just came in and shut the Angels down.

Cancel the résumés! Atlanta lost! But Toronto didn't, so we're still five back.

Sunday, September 1—NEW YORK

Twenty-four-year-olds aren't supposed to react to pressure the way that Don Mattingly does. The added pressure from the pennant race just seems to bring the best out of him.

Tonight, he hit two homers. The first one, in the sixth, narrowed California's lead to 3–2. His second one, in the seventh, was his twenty-fifth of the year and put us ahead 5–3, which we eventually wound up winning by.

Shirls got the win in relief. He took over for Cowls, who gave up five hits, seven walks, and three runs in just a little over five innings, his best outing in quite some time. Fish came on to get his tenth save by pitching a perfect two innings. The win brought us a game closer to Toronto, who lost to the White Sox.

Nancy called me this morning and told me that one of her friends from the West Coast had called her to tell her that there was a very interesting story about me in the *Los Angeles Times*. Supposedly, the story stated that Ted and I had already reached an agreement that would bring me back to Atlanta to manage the Braves. Which was totally untrue. Ted and I hadn't even talked about it.

But the real kicker is that it was also stated in the story that I had told Ted that I wouldn't agree to anything unless he promised to bring Joe back with me. Where do they come up with these stories?

Atlanta lost its second game in a row. This one by a whopping 15–2 score. If this keeps up, Ted may even consider signing my sixty-eight-year-old father just to get me back. Hell, from what I've seen, he's still got a better fastball than me. For that matter, so do both my mom and sister, Phyllis.

Rassy and Hudler were recalled from Columbus today. If his mind is with him, Rassy just might be that starting pitcher that we've been looking for.

Monday, September 2 — NEW YORK

They say that it's better to be lucky than good. Today was a prime example of that.

We scored four runs before the Mariners could even get anyone out. Then in the second inning, we scored three more to go ahead 7–0, which, with Guid on the mound, one would almost always automatically consider a game in the bag. Not true in this case. The Mariners came back and kicked our asses good in the fourth and fifth, and all of a sudden, we found ourselves up against the ropes.

So Billy brings in Allen to take over for Guid in the fifth. And Allen, who pitched so well the other day with a six-run lead, proved to be the Mariners biggest ally. After being totally unable to get anyone out, Allen left with us now leading by only a 7–6 score.

Thank God for small favors and slightly wild fastballs. Fish came in and literally saved the day, one that would have gone down as one of our most disastrous of the season. Fish went two and a third and struck out four while Rags finished up. We wound up winning, but we had to score another run in the seventh to do so.

Joe called me today and told me that the Yanks were interested in acquiring him. But right now it looks as if we don't stand a very good chance of getting Joe. The Astros are just asking too much. Supposedly, they want three minor leaguers: Scott Bradley, Jim Deshaies, and a young shortstop named Carlos Martinez. We're willing to give up the first two but not the third.

Right now, I guess that's the major difference between the Blue Jays and us. They're literally willing to mortgage their entire ball club just to get a shot at winning their first pennant. We're not.

I can't believe it! I mean, I'd never heard of anything like this ever happening before, let alone twice in a season. But it happened. The doctor that accidentally stabbed Billy in the lung in Texas, in July, got Willie Wilson today. Supposedly, the guy got Willie in the ass, which'll cause him to miss at least two or three weeks.

The one good thing that did come out of all this is the fact that we may have found a way to get Joe on the playoff roster, if we can get him and if we do win the pennant. All we gotta do is have all the bench jockeys get mandatory inoculations and have this guy give 'em. With the way he's goin' he's gotta put at least one of 'em on the D.L., which'll make room for Joe on the roster. It'll be kinda like a random drawing for who has to go. The first one screwed up goes on the D.L. Maybe they should start using this type of procedure for all roster moves? That doctor could make a bundle.

Tuesday, September 3 — NEW YORK

Tonight's game was a real big one for me, 'cause it basically set the stage for me to win No. 300 here against Toronto on the thirteenth.

Nobody wants to win the biggest game of their lives in a place like Cleveland or somethin' or against a team like the Indians or Mariners. Heck no! You want to win it at home, in front of a packed house and against the division leader in a pennant race. If I won it in a place like Cleveland, I'd be lucky if there were 7,000 fans in the stands, and half of them would probably be from my hometown.

Tonight's game was anything but a laugher. But like last night's game, it started out looking like one. Like last night, we jumped on Seattle's ass early by scoring five runs in the first, added another in the sixth and cruised in the seventh with a 6–0 lead.

But then that old polka injury crept up again in my back, and I knew that some shoulder problems would be following along shortly after. Sure enough, in the sixth my shoulder began throbbing and I loaded the bases real quick with only one out. Normally in a situation like this, Billy would be out of the dugout in a flash to yank me out of the game. But with our bullpen being as overworked as they were, he decided to leave me in.

I again got behind on the next guy real quick and was forced to come in with my hummer. Which hitters just wait on with the same enthusiasm a lion waits for the appearance of a deer. And as usually happens, the guy ripped the ball. This time to right field.

As the ball dove rapidly toward the ground, I just kept thinkin' to myself, "Dammit, Winnie, if you're ever gonna make a great play, make it now. Winnie caught the ball in stride and uncorked a perfect one-hopper right to Hass, who was then promptly bowled over by Alvin Davis, and sent sprawling across the home-plate area. He held onto the ball and saved my butt. I was out of the inning.

That was one of the great plays Hass made tonight. He was takin' knucklers and foul balls off the shoulder, mask, everywhere. All I could keep thinking to myself was what Ueck said about catching my knuckler when he first joined the Braves. "I met a lot of people when I was catchin' Phil's knuckleball," he said. "Unfortunately, all of 'em were behind home plate."

In the seventh, I again struggled and somehow got out of it without the Mariners scoring. But in the eighth I just didn't have anything left. But, yet, I still somehow got two guys out before I walked the bases full, and then walked in a few runs.

Then Billy put on one of the greatest exhibitions of acting I'd ever seen, comprising the greatest legal stall of all time, lasting nearly twelve minutes. Which began with no one warming up in the bullpen, and ended with Billy calling in Rags and then walking to the mound so slowly that he looked like he had a head-high case of hemorrhoids. Rags came in and saved my ever-lovin' Polish behind. We finally won 6–3, my fourteenth win of the season and the two hundred and ninety-eighth of my career. Setting the stage for me to win No. 299 against Oakland on Sunday and hopefully No. 300 against Toronto on the thirteenth.

I threw 157 pitches tonight. Either we've got to get another starter or I've gotta start gettin' paid by the pitch, just like Omar used to get paid by the at-bat.

Billy sensed that I was really hurtin', and after the game he came up to me and told me that if I wasn't able to pitch that he'd try to get me my last two wins out of the bullpen. Nice gesture on his part. But I just can't see how he'd be able to do that with us bein' in a pennant race and all.

Wednesday, September 4 — NEW YORK

Marty hurt his elbow so Billy was forced to start Rich Bordi tonight, who turned in a great performance. Bordi took us into the seventh with a 4–1 lead, which Allen quickly narrowed to 4–3. But it was the always-ready Shirls who came in to save the day with some stellar relief. In reward, Shirls got his first save since 1981, quite an accomplishment for a reliever as accomplished as Shirls.

Otis Nixon of the Indians, who used to be in Billy's shithouse when he was around here, hit a homer tonight to beat Toronto and bring us another game closer to the Jays.

"You know," said Billy after the game, with a real shit-eating grin on his face, "I always did like that Otis Nixon."

Thursday, September 5 — NEW YORK

This new video craze is driving everybody crazy, including George. Tonight, the first-base ump Ken Kaiser blew a call by calling Mike Davis of the A's safe on an infield single. George grew so incensed at what had happened that he called down and ordered the play to be replayed over and over and over and over again on the scoreboard, causing the umps to get so pissed off that they actually came over to Billy and threatened to pull themselves off the field. Which didn't bother Billy a whole hell of a lot, 'cause he kinda feels the game would be better without 'em anyway. In fact, he probably would have even worked as the sole arbitrator for the rest of the contest in their place, if they would have let him.

Besides George's role, Willie Randolph also played a significant role in our win tonight. He went four for four, with two homers, a double, and a single. Whit also looked good and got us through the sixth for his ninth win of the year. Toronto won again, though. So we're still two and a half back.

Friday, September 6 — NEW YORK

Cowls started today and got bombed, which has been happening a lot to him lately. So Super Shirls was called on to pitch in the second and wound up goin' the rest of the way, giving up only five hits and one run—and goin' farther than any starter has gone, with the exception of Guid and me, since August 26. That tells ya somethin' about our startin' staff.

Shirls deservedly got the win, off the strength of a seven-run fifth in which both Pasqua and Donny, who may just be the next Maris-Mantle tandem, both hit three-run homers.

The win was our seventh in a row and kept us within two and a half of Toronto, who won again.

Mom still hasn't gotten her hats. She'll probably drive up on the thirteenth to see me go after No. 300, if I can get past the A's on Sunday. George better have those hats waitin' for her at the hotel, or who knows what'll happen.

Saturday, September 7 — NEW YORK

Pete Rose has been talkin' a lot lately. One day he's attacking his ex-wife in the paper and the next day he's on Joe's and my ass. Today he was quoted as sayin', "I have over one hundred hits off the Niekro brothers. That's one-fortieth of my hits. I wish they'd a had triplets."

Guid won his eighteenth tonight as we beat the A's 3–2. But it was a game that we could have easily lost. We were out-hit 10–5. But it's the mark of a good team that can still win even when they're out-hit and out-played.

We scored the winning run on a wild one tonight. Knowing that we weren't hitting, Billy called a squeeze in the sixth, with Winnie at third. But having all the ex-Yankees on their club that they do, the A's were ready for it, called a pitchout and caught Winnie off third. But then they screwed up the rundown and Winnie wound up scoring.

Toronto lost today 6–3 to Minnesota, so we're now only one and a half out, the closest we've been to them since July.

Sunday, September 8 — NEW YORK

As I walked out to the bullpen to warm up before today's game, I hurt all over. No. 298 had really taken its toll on me. I can't ever remember being so tired. After the game, I actually doubted if I'd be able to pitch at all again this season.

The hurting stayed with me the entire week. I hurt everywhere. And as I walked out to the bullpen before the game tonight I really wondered if I was gonna be able to pitch or not. That old polka injury in my lower back was flaring up, which was makin' my hip hurt, which was makin' my leg throb, which made the entire right side of my back sore. To top it all off, my arm felt like a lead weight.

When I got out to the bullpen, Rassy was all ready to warm up in case I wouldn't be able to make it. Rags was standing around watchin' me. He could see that I was hurting. I gave him a quarter and I told him to toss it in the air.

"Heads, I give it a try," I said, "tails I let Rassy take a shot at it." He flipped the coin in the air, caught it, didn't even look at it, and then said, "Heads," then stuck the quarter in his pocket and walked away.

When I got out there tonight I was terrible. My fastball was slow, my slider didn't break, my screwball didn't screw, and my knuckler was just uncontrollable. I went just as far as my tired arm would take me, which was into the seventh. Thank God for small miracles. The bullpen held and I won No. 299 by a score of 9–6 over the A's.

It was great to win No. 299 and all. We were still within one and a half of the Jays, who beat the Twins by the score of 10–9.

Monday, September 9 — MILWAUKEE

Dale Berra had to go to Pittsburgh this week and testify in the Federal Court case concerning the drug scandal. When he got on the stand, Yog admitted first using cocaine at a New Year's Eve party in 1979 and then said that he continued to use it about once or twice a month for the next four years. Then he went on to say that the drug made him feel "euphoric."

They don't use that word in comic books, do they? 'Cause those are the only kinda books that Dale reads. Where could Yog have come up with that word then? Hell, no wonder he's been in a slump for the last six months. He's been working that long on coming up with a word to use to dazzle 'em in court.

I know one thing for sure, if Billy was a judge he sure as hell would have jailed his ass for that base-running blunder he pulled back in August. Nothing personal against Dale, mind you. Billy would have just done it for the betterment of the game.

Guid's been sayin' for the last few weeks that this team is good but isn't as good as the '78 team. He says the major difference between the two teams is that the '78 team had a killer instinct. I think they also played better in extra-inning games. Hell, we're only 6–10 so far this reason in extra-inning games, and that includes our win tonight. But I think a lot of our problem is the age of some of our best players. We've just got a couple of essential old guys that usually fall asleep by the end of the ninth.

Tonight Marty started and got lit up. He lasted only four and two-thirds before Billy had to go to his trusty bullpen once again and herd in a parade of relievers. Shirls was first, then Fish, and then Rags, and we went into the tenth tied with the Brewers 4–4.

That's when we exploded for five runs, featuring a tie-breaking two-run single by Pags, who had four hits tonight. He's really starting to come into his own.

Tuesday, September 10 — MILWAUKEE

What the Metrodump is to artificial turf, the Milwaukee County Stadiumdump is to natural grass. Last night Willie Randolph pulled his hamstring playin' on this field, which was still wet from Sunday night's rain. When Billy asked one of the groundskeepers why they didn't put the tarp on to keep the field dry when it rained Sunday night, the guy said that it had a hole in it.

Tonight, Whit got mauled for twelve hits and eight runs in only seven innings. To show you how good our hitters are, Whit still won the game, his tenth of the year. With his ERA, there's no other team in the big leagues with which he could have won ten games this year. But with us, he sometimes looks like a pretty good pitcher.

Tonight, it was a five-run fifth, a four-run fourth and a three-run eighth—and the help of Shirls, who got his second save of the season—that won it for us.

Pete Rose broke Ty Cobb's record today. And one of the nicest aspects of his feat was that he did it in his hometown of Cincinnati. I know how he feels about winning it in Cincinnati 'cause I kinda wish that I could win No. 300 where it all started for me too, back in beautiful Lansing, Ohio, home of the Blaine Coalmine, Fritz's Barbershop and the Melody Manor.

And George probably wouldn't mind me winning it there either. In fact, he might even encourage me to do so, being that he'd probably be worried that something might backfire and go wrong, and I'd end up actually winning No. 300 against the Yanks at the stadium or somethin'.

But I already checked into the availability of the local legion field, and there's no way I could arrange to get it. They're all booked up with little gridder games until way past the end of the season.

I was gonna send Pete a telegram from both Joe and me congratulating him on accomplishing his feat. But the truth is that I was kinda hurt by the fact that neither I nor Joe ever got one from him thanking us for helping him so much through the years. Hell, if it wasn't for me, that forty-four-game hitting streak of his would've only gone forty-three games!

As far as Joe and I are concerned, playing our substantial part in Pete's record-breaking feat was worth it. Just to know that we played a big part in causing one of the toughest guys to ever play the game to cry is enough of a thank-you for us.

Toronto won again. They beat Detroit 2–1. So we're still one and a half back.

Wednesday, September 11— MILWAUKEE

We got screwed out of a win tonight when umpire Vic Voltaggio made a lousy call on a foul ball in the ninth that allowed the

Brewers to score the winning run. Heck, everybody in the stadium could see it was foul. But, unfortunately, Voltaggio was the one makin' the call.

Up until Voltaggio blew it, we'd hung in there pretty well. Cowls went seven, and even though the Brewers were hittin' him pretty good, they'd only scored three runs. While we, on the other hand, had to bust our asses to get three off this kid named Higuera that the Brewers had pitching for them. Right now, I'd say that Higuera is the best young left-hander in the league. Anybody who holds our guys to only three runs and six hits over nine with the way they're hittin' has got to be.

But, unfortunately, the game came down to one lousy call, a call that dropped us another game behind the Jays, as we enter our series against them this week in New York.

George has been bustin' his ass to get Tom Seaver from the White Sox. But the Sox just want too much. Right now they're askin' for Hass and a starting pitcher. George has also been checking into getting Moose Haas from the Brewers. But they want Pasqua. As far as Joe is concerned, that deal seems to be dead too. They still want three minor leaguers, and George is offering only two.

As far as Seaver is concerned, if it were a month earlier and it looked like Seaver was gonna win No. 300 at the stadium, I bet you wouldn't hear George sayin' that the Sox were askin' too much. No, in fact, I think that if he had to do it over again, he would've paid just about any price to get Seaver into pinstripes back then.

Thursday, September 12 — NEW YORK

They're calling today Super Thursday in New York 'cause the Mets play the Cardinals over at Shea this afternoon, and we play the Jays here tonight. But as far as I'm concerned, it's more like Suicide Thursday. 'Cause I'd just as soon walk as risk my life by riding on one of those goddamn trains from Flushing to here.

It was the perfect match-up tonight: Guid versus Stieb. But the game wound up being won not by one of these two superstars, but by Babe Hassey, whose three-run dinger accounted for the last three runs in our six-run seventh.

Though Guid wasn't his usual dominating self, he was good enough to get the win, while Fish came in and pitched the last inning for his twelfth save.

We're now within one and a half of the Jays. But if it weren't for Voltaggio's call, we may have been only a half game out. What an extra bit of incentive that would have been for me to win No. 300, knowing that it would put us into first place.

There's this guy from Eastern Sports Programming Network named Chris Berman who's always all over Hass. Berman must have seen Hass play regularly with the Indians.

The other night Hass hit a dinger and Berman described it for the viewing audience as some type of revelation. But it was his eleventh of the year. That's a career high for Hass. I admit that Hass is no Yogi Berra, but he's the best we've got right now and he's having a hell of a year.

Finally, tonight, Berman gave Hass some credit by labeling him as an unsung hero. But heck, Hass had to hit one into the upper deck to get Berman to acknowledge him as anything other than a former Indian.

We purchased Rod Scurry from the Pirates today. He's a left-handed reliever with a wicked curveball. With all the talent he possesses, he comes ready equipped with a whole long line of problems. Kinda like a left-handed throwing Neil Allen.

Though I realize that we probably got him to take Shirl's place in the bullpen, he's still not what we need. We need a legitimate starting pitcher. One that would get us into the later innings each start, a guy that wouldn't tax our bullpen as heavily as some of the other guys have been doin'.

Right now, our bullpen's really draggin'. But they're all that's holding us together at this point. If they go, we go too.

Friday, September 13 — NEW YORK

The stadium was already packed tonight when I walked out to the bullpen. There had to be at least 50,000 fans here tonight, or about twice as many as showed up to see me polka a month or so ago. As Bill Monboquette walked with me out to the bullpen, I told him that I just couldn't believe it.

"If someone had told me 25 years ago, or even two years ago," I said, "that I'd be walkin' out to the Yankee bullpen on a Friday the thirteenth to get ready to pitch for my three hundredth victory, in front of an overflow crowd, and in a game that could bring us within half a game of first place, I would have told them that they were full of shit."

It all was a dream come true for me. I just couldn't believe it. I mean, the last few years had been somewhat like a dream come true for me. Yeah, there'd been a few nightmares too. I hear those are quite frequent around here, but tonight all I could think of was the good times, both of 'em, to be exact. My family was all here, my friends, everybody that I really cared about in the world, except for my dad, who couldn't make the trip. But like with every game that I pitched, I dedicated it to him in my heart, whether he was here or not.

I was caught up in all the excitement, pageantry, and the pennant race. I didn't have any more aches and pains. Our trainers had seen to that. They'd just transplanted my head onto the body of a twenty-five-year-old, or that's what it felt like. I felt so young and fired up.

I went out there and pitched my ass off, my best game of the season. I went the full nine, struck out five, and didn't give up any earned runs. Unfortunately, two costly errors, one by Hass and the other by Don Mattingly, allowed three unearned runs to cross the plate, and we wound up losing by a score of 3–2.

George was the first guy to greet me as I came into the clubhouse. He compassionately shook my hand and told me that I should have won.

Ya know, I never really ever thought about Friday the thirteenth being any different from any of the other 364 days of the year.

But with the way I pitched tonight and with the way we played and still lost, I may have to reconsider.

Willie's pulled hamstring has been really botherin' him. Billy knows it, too, and tried to get him to take himself out of the lineup tonight, but Willie refused.

"Not while we're playin' Toronto," he said. "I can rest after that. We all can."

But the decision to play Willie may have cost us the game tonight, or at least a much better chance of winning it. It seems that whenever a player has a key injury, like Willie, in an important game, like tonight, the player's injury somehow comes into play in a crucial way.

In the second Willie walked and was on first when Meach drilled a ball to left. Running all the way, Meach's hit should have been a for sure triple. Unfortunately, when Meach slid into third, Willie was still standing there. Luckily, Meach was able to bolt back to second to avoid being tagged out. But in a normal circumstance that wouldn't have happened 'cause Willie would have scored easily. In fact, almost any of us could have scored from first on Meach's hit, including yours truly.

But instead of Meach tying up the game with his base hit, we got nothin', 'cause Hendy, the next batter, popped up. That may have been the turning point of the game for us right there.

Saturday, September 14 — NEW YORK

Billy took Willie's name out of the lineup tonight and put Hudler in his place. Willie was real pissed and protested all the way, but Billy was right. A healthy guy out there last night might have won the game for us. And bein' three and a half back, we couldn't afford to drop another game this weekend.

Billy started Shirls tonight and just prayed for another good game from him, but this time it didn't come. Though they only got two runs off of him, they beat up Shirls pretty bad, and Billy was forced to bring in Rags in the sixth to try and keep the game close. Unfortunately, Rags just lost it. He faced four guys, didn't get any of 'em out, walking one and giving up hits to the other three. All four wound up scoring. By the time he left, we were trailing 7–2.

We've been depending too much on our bullpen. Rags was just too tired out there. Those guys can't afford to make a mistake. They're asked to come in by the fifth inning almost every night. And if they make even one single mistake, even that early in the contest, it usually costs us the game. Such as what happened tonight. But Rags has nothing to be ashamed of, he and the rest of the guys out there have done more than any manager could ever ask for them to do. We just need another starting pitcher or two.

We wound up losin' tonight, which kinda drove everything into a frenzy. George, who wants to win this thing as much as anybody, started complainin' in the press box about how bad we were goin'. Every man has his right to his opinion, but I wish he would have remained silent for a little while longer. The last thing we needed was him puttin' more pressure on us.

I guess that he just walked into the press box, obviously looking for a direct confrontation with the media, and started screaming at the top of his lungs for Reggie Jackson. "Where's Reggie Jackson," he yelled. "We need a Mr. October or a Mr. September."

Then he started getting on our hitters. "My big guys aren't coming through—Winfield, Baylor, Griffey. They're letting us down. That's a fact."

George was especially hard on Winnie. He referred to him for the press as "Mr. May." I'm not one to tell George how to run his ball club, but we really don't need this criticism from him right now.

Winnie, who's got a lotta of balls and who also has a long-term contract, is used to battling George through the media. He was about the only one of us that wasn't afraid to confront George via the press. He told it like it is.

"There's a feeling among us that we'd like to tell him, 'Shut up. You don't know what you're talking about.'" Amen.

· · ·

Mr. May drove in his one hundredth RBI of the season tonight. He's having another great year. In fact, he's the first Yankee to drive in 100 RBI's for four consecutive years since Yogi Berra did it in the early fifties. And if Baylor keeps hitting the way he is, we'll end up with three guys with one hundred-RBI seasons.

Tom Boswell of the *Washington Post*, looking for a few juicy quotes, went up to George after the game and asked him a few questions, one of which had to do with Billy's decision to use Rags so early in the game.

George had a suggestion of his own to make to Boswell. "Ask Billy why he brought in Dave Righetti in the fifth inning, "but don't say who told you to do so." George had a little somethin' to say about everybody today. But then he had reason to, 'cause we're playing horseshit.

This battle between the Jays and us has almost turned into an international confrontation. It all began when some Canadian newspapers started bad-mouthing us for just being American. It must be an old hockey tactic or somethin'. Of course, they can do that on the ice rink, where they're clearly superior; but who wouldn't be after growing up in a freezer? But on the diamond, they're clearly inferior. It must be all that ale they drink that gives these false visions of grandeur.

Well, the other night our fans, who'd caught wind of some of the stories circulating around the Yukon, booed the Canadian National Anthem. Which I heard really pissed off a lot of Canadian officials. But what are they gonna do about it, cut off our ale supply? Or cut off our orders for bearskin coats?

Then tonight, Mary O'Dowd, who was scheduled to sing the respective anthems, began singing the Canadian rendition and then stopped halfway through because she'd forgotten the words. It was the most bizarre thing that I'd ever heard. She had to run into our dugout to get a copy of the words and then run back out to the microphone and start again.

Her miscue couldn't have come at a worse time. I hear the Canadians are really pissed. I can imagine how they feel. I'm sure it's tough being considered a colony of the United States. I hear they're so pissed about what happened that they're considering sending an official anthem singer on the road with both the Jays and Expos so a miscue like Ms. O'Dowd's never happens again.

Sunday, September 15 — NEW YORK

Whit was the guy on the hot seat today. I bet Billy even considered trying to get ahold of Bo Derek—and pay for her to fly in for the game. That's about the only thing that's worked with Whit this season, outside of Mark Connor. But unfortunately, Mark's been gone for over a month and a half. And since he was fired, Whit has gone back to pitching like he was at the beginning of the season.

But he's been real fortunate, and we were hopin' that some of that luck was gonna surface today. Heck, in one stretch earlier this month, he pitched in twenty-three innings and gave up twenty-two runs. But yet, he wound up with a 1–0 record in those games. And in the other four games involved in that stretch, even though he didn't get a decision, we wound up winning. A 8.59 ERA over five games and a 1–0 record. He should just feel fortunate to be in the big leagues with stats like that.

Though he narrowly escaped being buried in the first two innings today, the Jays jumped on Whit and then Rassy for six runs. Billy had to dig deep into our exhausted bullpen again. Even Scurry and Army, who was recalled on September 5, got a chance to pitch. But we still ended up losing, though we rallied gallantly in the later innings. Our pennant hopes appear to be dashed.

George pulled his press-box routine again today. I hear that he was really pissed. He has a reason to be, 'cause we were terrible. But I think that sometimes he forgets that we have feelings too, and that we're real professionals, who hurt worse than anything when they blow an important series like this. Right now, we're lower than worm shit.

We finally got us another starting pitcher, Joe. George was finally able to work that trade through with the Astros. Unfortunately, right now, it may be too late.

. . .

Baylor finally got tired of everything around here and asked to be traded. I can't blame him. He's one of the top hitters in the game, and it frustrates the shit out of him when he doesn't get to play. Heck, he started only one game this weekend, and he's got nearly 100 RBI's. Pasqua started the other three.

Don Mattingly summed it up best today, when he described the present situation with the club as simply "out of control."

Monday, September 16 — NEW YORK

Billy's not happy with the way George has been attacking both us and his managerial decisions, and he's begun to respond in some very strange and detrimental ways. I thought that Billy knew George better than that by now. Though George's methods are different, and in this case ineffective, that's just his way of motivating people. He just believes that the best way to get someone to do something is to jump on their ass.

Unfortunately, George may have pissed Billy off too much this time. 'Cause Billy has gotten really crazy with some of his thoughts and actions. Tonight, for example, I think that in direct retaliation to George's statements about him bringing Rags into the game too early on Saturday, Billy left Fish in the game way too long.

Billy just doesn't like anyone, including the guy signing his paycheck, telling him how to run his ball club. And I think his actions tonight were his way of trying to ram that point home with George. Unfortunately, Fish got racked for six runs, and we lost the game as a result. A game, now that we're five back of Toronto, we sure could've used.

Some of the reporters went into Billy's office after the game and—as I'm sure Billy saw it—had the balls to question his decision about leaving Fish in for so long.

He just screamed in reply to their questions, "I didn't want to blow out my bullpen." But that never seemed to enter his mind before, or ever stop him from dipping three or four relievers deep into the bullpen at any other time this year.

Tuesday, September 17—DETROIT

I think that Billy either already believes he's gone or wants to be gone. Maybe he's just tired of all the pressure around here, too? 'Cause tonight, he pulled another one, something totally uncharacteristic of him, when he's in his right mind. In fact, his decision almost looked premeditated. Maybe he really does want out of here.

Again, his actions involved another pitcher. This time it was the ace of our staff, Guid, who Billy has helped nurture almost Guid's entire career.

Well, tonight Billy just stood there and watched as Guid, obviously not his overpowering self, hung himself on the mound. Not until the Tigers had rapped him for five dingers and seven runs, and not until the game was well out of reach, did Billy come to his aid. And then, when he finally did come to his rescue, he didn't exactly throw him a life preserver; he instead threw him an anchor in the form of Rassy, who is just not a very good relief pitcher.

I think for the first time since I got here, Rags is in Billy's shithouse, basically on the premise that he failed to close the doors on the Jays last Saturday. Why else would he have used Rassy before him. I realize that the game was already out of reach, but if he had brought Rags in to replace Guid a few innings earlier, it may not have been.

We lost 9–1 and are still five back of Toronto, who lost to Boston.

The ceremonial flip of the coins was conducted today between the first two teams in each division of the American League for the right to see who gets the homefield advantage should one or both of the divisions finish in a dead heat. Toronto won out over us, and K.C. got the nod over California.

Though outwardly no one seemed to give a shit, there is still a quiet optimism floating around here, a hope that we'll get another crack at the Jays in the final weekend of the season. But unfortunately, the pennant race seems out of our hands at the present moment. All we can do is try to win each one of our remaining games and just hope that the Jays lose a few.

Wednesday, September 18 — DETROIT

I pitched like a forty-six-year-old tonight, but Billy let me finish the entire game. But I'm sure that he did so hoping that we would come back and score enough runs for me to get my three hundredth. But such was not the case. We lost 5–2 and missed an opportunity to pick up a game on Toronto, who lost to Boston again.

Everyone either flew in or drove in to see me pitch tonight, all my relatives, neighbors from home and close friends. Ninety-two of 'em in all. About the only one that didn't make it was George. But he called earlier in the afternoon to tell me that he wouldn't be able to make it because he was tied up in court. Which was O.K. with me, because then I wouldn't have to leave him a ticket. I'd already sponged enough comp tickets off the guys to put me butt-deep in debt for the rest of the season.

In his most bizarre move of the week, Billy ordered Pags, normally a left-handed hitter, to bat right-handed for the first time in his career. All this madness took place in the sixth inning, with the score tied and the go-ahead run on third base. Pags had struck out against Mickey Mahler, who has a big, sweeping curveball, twice already. In his third trip to the plate, this one from the right-hand side, he went down looking.

Said Pags after the game, "I felt comfortable up there. I just couldn't pull the trigger." Yeah, but you looked funny as hell. I wonder if Billy really does want out of here, or if he's just playin' games with George's mind?

Thursday, September 19 — DETROIT

Joe made his first start as a Yankee tonight and got his ever-lovin' Polish sausage knocked off. Thank God Billy didn't allow him to dangle from the end of his own rope too long, though.

The Tigers got Joe for six runs and seven hits in only one and two thirds before Billy brought in Scurry to replace him, who was followed by a parade of others, namely Allen, Rassy, and Armstrong. Yes, Mike Armstrong. Army pitched great again tonight. He went two innings without allowing a hit. Since Rags is now in the shithouse, maybe Billy's grooming Army to take his place as the stopper? Well then again, *naaaawwwww*, I don't think Billy would do that. He was probably just heaping further punishment on Rags, by making him watch Army pitch in his spot.

We're now five and a half behind Toronto.

Michael Spinks, who's scheduled to fight Larry Holmes later this year, was quoted in the paper today as saying, "I'm going to be trying like a man lost on the moon trying to get back to earth." I think that's how most of us feel about this pennant race. Even with all the confusion around here, we still haven't given up yet. We're still livin' for that one final crack at the Jays.

Friday, September 20 — BALTIMORE

Whit was our scheduled starter today, but Billy scratched his name from the lineup card before the game. He said that he did so because Whit was suffering from some arm trouble. But Whit was really pissed off, 'cause he said that he wasn't having any arm trouble. In fact, he said that he never felt better.

I think the truth of the matter is that Whit has just been pitching terrible lately, and Billy was punishing him for his poor outing against the Jays on Sunday. Include Whit in Billy's Shithouse Crew now, too. But then Billy may have just wanted to give Rich Bordi another chance to start, since he pitched so well his last time out.

Either way, Billy's got one real pissed off Tennessean on his hands. Not only is Whit mad, but he's also embarrassed. Nobody likes to be shown up like that, especially when everyone knows that the reason Billy gave for scratchin' him was very questionable. I'm not sayin' that Whit could have taken Billy being honest any better. But at least he would have respected him for it.

. . .

Just when I thought that things couldn't get any more bizarre, they have. Tonight, we lost the game because Billy went to his nose at the wrong time. That's right, went to his nose at the wrong time.

Billy's got this signal for when he wants the pitcher to pitch out. He simply rubs his nose. Well, tonight, with the score tied 2–2 in the seventh inning, Lee Lacy batting with a 2–0 count, two out, and Alan Wiggins on first, Billy accidentally gave Butch the pitch-out sign. Unfortunately, there was no need for it. Wiggins wasn't goin'. The pitchout ran the count to 3–0.

Bordi's next pitch was a ball, walking Lacy to first and putting Wiggins in scoring position at second. Cal Ripken, who was the next batter up, then got a base hit that scored Wiggins.

Billy's got to get these signals right. The right index finger in the right nostril should mean to keep the runner close. While the same index finger in the left nostril should mean pitchout. While a left index finger, or any other finger for that matter, thumb and toes included stuck in a nostril should nullify anything and just serve as a decoy.

We wound up losing the game 4–2. It was our eighth loss in a row and dropped us to six and a half behind Toronto.

Saturday, September 21—BALTIMORE

Billy has been really down lately, but that doesn't stop him from goin' down to the hotel bar to have a few drinks after the game. Tonight, there was a newly-wed couple and a bunch of their friends sitting across the bar from Billy in the hotel. Billy sent them over a bottle of champagne.

A few minutes later, they invited him over for a drink and a nice conversation ensued. In fact, I think that it was a good distraction for Billy. He may have even forgot how bad things were goin' on the field for him. He just sat there jokin' and laughin' with the folks for quite some time, before returning to his place at the bar.

But about a half-hour later, the groom came storming over to Billy, grabbed Billy by the arm and tried to drag him outside. Billy just tried to brush him off, but the guy just kept comin' after him.

Finally, the guy started screaming at Billy, accusing him of saying that his bride had a potbelly. But Billy corrected him politely by pointing at the other couple who was sitting with the newlyweds, the woman in the couple especially, and claiming that he hadn't insulted the guy's wife but had merely made reference to the girth of the other lady at their table. Or, as Billy said, "her fat ass."

But the guy just wouldn't leave Billy be. Finding it impossible to believe that Billy had not made reference to his wife's potbelly, he just started screamin', "I just married her this afternoon," as if that should have anything to do with her potbelly or the fat ass of the lady sitting with them.

Right then and there, Billy got up from his seat and tried to walk away from the guy and out of the bar. But the guy persisted and some shoving started. In seconds, the bartenders had a full-fledged fight on their hands. But in no time at all, and with some help from some of our guys in the bar, the two were separated, with Billy, who was as mad as a hornet, being restrained by several of the guys.

"All I can say," said Billy, "is he caught me right. I was in the perfect mood. I'll tell you this: I didn't get to him, but I sure as hell wanted to."

We finally won tonight. Hass, Cowls, who started, and Griff were the big heros. Well, at least I hope beating Weaver and his Orioles will brighten Billy up. Toronto won, though, so we're still six and a half back.

Sunday, September 22 — BALTIMORE

Billy was sitting in the hotel bar again tonight, the scene of last night's caper, with Yog and his wife, having a few drinks when some guy came over and said, "Whitson's in trouble."

So Billy and Yog raced across the room, supposedly to rescue Whit. But when they got there, they found that Whit wasn't the one in need of assistance. The guy who Whit had stood up in the corner and was choking was the one that needed the assistance.

Supposedly, Billy tried to pull Whit off the guy, and that's when Whit turned on Billy and started flailin' anything and everything in his direction. Yog immediately came to Billy's defense and landed a punch on Whit's lip, Yog's first hit since May.

Billy, never one to shy away from such a flurry, grabbed Whit and wrestled him to the floor. The two men, both cursing and screaming at each other, were quickly separated. But the fight resumed a few minutes later, after the two were dragged outside to the lobby. Then Whit did something that a lot of Billy's colleagues through the years and old girlfriends were probably envious of. He kicked Billy right square in the nuts.

"He got me a good one," admitted Billy.

Whit's next kick broke Billy's right arm. I think Billy was surprised by Whit's assault.

"I can't fight feet," he claimed. "Maybe I ought to go to one of those karate schools."

Shit, I wish I would've known about that earlier. I'm a pretty fair two-stepper ya know. It's all that early polka training.

Whit was whisked out of the hotel, put on a plane as fast as possible, and flown home to New Jersey. Initially, Billy claimed that Whit would never pitch for him again. But he softened his stance once the pain from the kick in the groin resided.

"I don't have to like him," he said. "If he can help us win the pennant, I'll pitch him. And I'll yank him from the mound, too, if he has to be yanked, but this time I'll watch his feet."

Guid won his twentieth tonight, and Billy let Rags out of the shithouse to save it for him. We just looked like the Yankees of old tonight. There seems to be a new enthusiasm about the team. It's a lot different than how playin' Billyball feels. I think what we're feelin' is more like Billy*brawl*.

We picked up a game on the Jays, so we're now only five and a half out.

Tuesday, September 24 — NEW YORK

I'm getting tired of letting people down, the fans, my family, friends, George, myself. Tonight, I went out there and pitched my duppa off and ended up getting kicked right in the rocks. The

Tigers got me again. I wonder what they've got against me? Don't they have any respect for their elders?

Last night was Joe's first day in New York with the team, so we went out and I showed him the sights. We dragged in sometime in the middle of the night. Nonetheless, I was still feelin' real fresh and strong when I took the mound tonight. That didn't seem to matter, though, 'cause the Tigers got me for eight runs and seven hits in only four innings.

I was really pissed as I walked off the field and into the dugout. When I get like this at home, which is rare, I go out in the back yard and chop wood. Instead, tonight, I just grabbed a fungo bat on the way back toward the clubhouse and beat the living shit out of a pay phone.

George and Winnie are still goin' at it. Today George came into the clubhouse and was gonna distribute some letters to the players from the commissioner on drug testing. It's normally Winnie's job to do such things, and he ran up to George and grabbed the letters out of his hands.

"I'll take those and distribute them," Winnie said, glaring right at George. "I'm the player rep on this team. It's my job. This is my team in that regard."

That's all Winnie had to say to George to get his dander up. All I could think of is, "Boy are we in for some fireworks around here now!"

George just glared back and said, "Not for long. I'm the boss around here. We'll see if you're going to be around next season."

Winnie just replied with all the confidence of a man with a long-term, no-trade contract, "You know where I'm going to be next season? I'm going to be right here."

I wonder if we can get a Professional Wrestling card billed around a match between these two. I'd certainly buy at least a dozen tickets.

Wednesday, September 25 — NEW YORK

Joe's six years younger than I. Plus, he had an extra day to recuperate from our outing the other night. No wonder he pitched a hell of a lot better tonight then I did yesterday.

Although he only lasted five innings, he had allowed only one run. He had to leave because he took a line drive off the shin. Shit, everybody's gettin' beat up around here. But Fish and Scurry were able to come in and close the door, as we won 10–2.

It was Joe's first win for the Yankees. Another reason to go out and celebrate tonight. That and Toronto lost again. We're now only six out.

It looks like Billy is gone and that George is just gonna let him finish out the season. Hell, the press isn't even talkin' about Billy being fired anymore. They talk like it's already happened. They've even got our new manager named already—Lou Piniella.

I think that the only way that we can save Billy's job for him is to win the pennant. But the question is, after all the shit he's put up with, does he really want his job saved?

Thursday, September 26, HURRICANE-OUT — NEW YORK

The big question around here was which would happen first, the firing of Billy or hurricane Gloria hitting. Gloria won.

Friday, September 27, HURRICANE-OUT — NEW YORK

Billy did it again. He went over George's head and cancelled our workout. Hurricane or no hurricane, there was no way that Billy was gonna endure the rain and the seventy-five-mile-per-hour winds to spend an afternoon watching us run through mud puddles.

Saturday, September 28 — NEW YORK

Mom called Joe and me before the game today. Dad's sick, real sick. He's got an aneurysm in his stomach. It doesn't look good.

The doctors told mom that they'd have to operate immediately, if they were to have any chance of saving him.

And in his poor physical condition, they'll have to do a complete blood transfusion and everything. They're only giving him a fifteen percent chance of making it through the operation. We took the first flight that we could to Pittsburgh. Then we'd drive from there into Wheeling, where my dad was.

The combination of the pennant race and George's insults have really got Winnie fired up. He's a natural born leader, as he proved again tonight. Pressure situations just seem to bring out the best of him.

Tonight, it was his two-out base hit in the ninth that drove in the winning run over the Orioles. Earlier in the game, he hit his twenty-fifth homer of the year and scored his one hundredth run, for the second consecutive year. That makes him the first Yankee to do that since Mantle did it in '60 and '61. Not bad for a Mr. May, huh?

Guid went the whole way tonight for his twenty-first win of the season, which leads the league. Though the win didn't bring us any closer to Toronto, who beat the Brewers, at least we didn't lose any ground. We're still six back.

Sunday, September 29 — NEW YORK

Joe and I were at the hospital to see my dad come out of the operating room. Then they wheeled him into intensive care. What a frightening sight, seeing all those tubes running in and out of him and hearing the sound of that respirator constantly humming in the background.

It was a real tough day for all of us. Things are still real touch and go. The doctors are still really surprised that he's even made it this far. Both Joe and I broke down a few times today. Just seeing him like that is really hard for us to take.

But by the end of the day, dad started to come around, which astounded everyone. Again, they didn't think that he'd make it that far. But he's still in real serious condition. Everything is still touch and go, so much so that Joe and I felt that it would be best to spend the night on the couches in the waiting room rather than to go back to the hotel.

Billy and Weaver are constantly trying to outdo each other. Today, Weaver, whose club is hopelessly out of the pennant race, got himself tossed outta both games, the second one even before it began. As if to say "Take that!" to Billy, who he knows doesn't have the same luxury because of our position in the pennant race.

We went on to win both games anyway. Maybe Earl just didn't want to stay around to see that happen? We've beat him so many times already this year.

Winnie was the big hero again. God, just think of how potent he would've been if George had challenged him even further by calling him Mr. April, or even Mr. January! Both he and Baylor hit two-run homers in the second game, to give us the sweep. Billy again started Bordi. He pitched well and won the second game, while Scurry came in and got his first save with three innings of no-hit relief.

Cowls won the first game. He looked like his old self again, too. He went seven and gave up only two hits before giving way to Rags, who got his twenty-seventh save of the year.

All in all, our pitchers gave up only six hits on the day. That's the kind of startin' pitching that we've been needing for a long time. Toronto won again, though, so we only picked up a half-game on 'em. But whatever, as long as we've got a chance to win it in the last weekend, no matter how slim that chance might be, that's what we've got to hope for. It's all that we've got left.

Monday, September 30 — NEW YORK

My father's condition caused me to lose all conception of time and place. I didn't even remember that I was supposed to pitch against the Orioles tonight until my mom asked me if I was gonna be flyin' back to New York.

At first, it didn't matter, nothin' seemed to matter. All that I could think of was my dad lying in that hospital. But then I began to realize that if I didn't go back, that I'd be letting a lot of other guys, my teammates, down too. I got a copy of the morning paper and read that we had swept the Orioles yesterday. We were still in the pennant race. They're still depending on me to be there.

I fumbled around with my decision for a couple of hours, until it came to the point where if I didn't make one quick, it would be made for me. Because I wouldn't be able to get a flight back anyway.

I decided to go in and talk to my dad about it. He was conscious. Though he couldn't talk, because they had a tube stuck in his throat so he could breath. But he could, at times, scribble a few words on a piece of paper.

I went in and stood before him and tried to explain the situation. He seemed to understand what I was trying to ask him. But it was so hard seeing him like this that I almost started to cry. Joe came in and just put his arm around me for support.

Immediately after I was done posing my question to him concerning whether I should fly back or stay, he tried to mouth his answer to me but nothing came out. Realizing this he tried to give me a sign with his hands. I walked across the room and got him a small tablet and a pencil and put it on the table leaning over his bed in front of him.

He started to write, but it came out like chicken scratching. I deciphered the first word as WIN. He kept writing. Three more words slowly appeared—I'LL BE HAPPY. That was his answer. Like only my father could give it.

Then he got this glow in his eyes, the type of glow that then and there I knew I would want to remember him by, and then he began shoving me away with his right hand. He wanted me to go, and go now. Right then and there I realized that the best thing that I could do for him was to get my butt back to New York and win No. 300. That more than anything else would help him. But before leaving, I tore the little piece of paper off the tablet and stuck it in my pocket.

Joe and I got on the next flight back to New York. We went straight to the ball park and arrived around five o'clock. By that time everybody, the press, Billy, everybody, was wonderin' if I was gonna show for the game tonight. Joe took care of talkin' to the press while I got ready for the game.

I stuck the slip of paper into the back pocket of my uniform just before I left to head out to the bullpen. When I got out there, I pulled it out of my pocket and sat down to look at it. I just kept thinking to myself, "God, if there's ever one game that I want to win, it's this one."

I went out there tonight and pitched with every bit of strength that I could muster. And when times got tough, I reached into my back pocket and pulled out the slip of paper and read the four words on it: WIN—I'LL BE HAPPY.

I gave it my all, but that wasn't enough. The Orioles touched me up for twelve hits and four runs. When Billy came out to the mound, he was fully aware of how much this game meant to me. I wasn't in there bustin' my balls just for victory No. 300 or for the team, I was pitching with a more defined purpose. I was pitchin' for my dad, the guy who'd taught me to throw the knuckleball and the guy who had been my coach and biggest fan through hundreds of high-school and legion games, thousands of pick-up games and twenty years in the big leagues.

We eventually came back and won it when Donny hit a two-run homer in the ninth, to tie it. Then Baylor drove in Winnie, who was the winning run. I was glad that we had won and happy that we had picked up another game on the Jays, but I was sad that I hadn't been able to win it for my dad.

Surprisingly, Weaver decided to stay around for this one. But I think he only did so because he had a 4–2 lead going into the ninth inning.

Tuesday, October 1—NEW YORK

After yesterday's game, I could have flown back to the hospital, either right after the game or early this morning, but I decided to stay 'cause I felt that Joe, who was scheduled to start tonight, would need the support. I thought that it was the least I could do. He'd always been there for me and we were going through this thing together, like we'd gone through so many other things in our lives.

Joe went out there and did a whole hell of a lot better job than I did, though. He shut the Brewers down almost all of the first six innings, until Billy had to go to the bullpen and fetch Rags, who shut 'em down the rest of the way for his twenty-eighth save.

The win was our sixth in a row, and it couldn't have come at a better time. 'Cause the Blue Jays lost tonight to the Tigers, who have been real ass-kickers during this pennant race. Ask me, I know. Right now, Toronto's magic number is at three, and holding.

I think Winnie, who's rapidly becoming our official team spokesman, best expressed our chances of winning the pennant when he said that they had gone from "bleak to dark." But right now that's all we could hope for and all that we're living for.

Wednesday, October 2 — NEW YORK

The word from the hospital was that dad was progressing quite well, but that he was still in intensive care. I was feeling a hell of a lot better today when I got up than I was on Monday.

I seemed to have a renewed vigor for life. I began seeing my start on Sunday against the Jays as even a bigger and better chance for me than last Monday had been. Mom said that already my dad was looking forward to me startin' against the Jays.

Everything just seemed to fall into place. I, myself, couldn't have designed a better day for me to win No. 300. If I was lucky, a win on Sunday could either tie us with the Jays for the pennant or win it for us. That was, of course, if we continued to play well this week.

Unfortunately, that young lefty from the Brewers, Higuera, shut us out, which reduced Toronto's magic number to two. Which means that we could be eliminated as early as tomorrow. Which would make me pitching against the Jays on Sunday a moot point. And that's not the way I had hoped to win No. 300, either for myself, or for my dad.

The real shame about tonight was that Shirls, again put into a tough situation, pitched a great game and gave up only four hits and one run, the only run scoring on a triple by a kid named Ready that trickled off the tip of a diving Winnie's glove and rolled to the wall. And that's no laughing matter.

Thursday, October 3 — NEW YORK

There was no nervousness, only determination and confidence in the clubhouse tonight. That's the only way a team in our circumstance could approach tonight's game. We could be eliminated tonight, but it would take two things: a loss by us coupled with a win by Toronto.

We were determined to do our part and take the pennant race, still intact, no matter how slim our hopes would be, to Toronto. It didn't matter whether their magic number was one or two going into the series, it really didn't matter. All we knew was that we had to win our four remaining games of the season to at least tie for the pennant.

Realizing the importance of each game, this one tonight being the most important of all, Billy sent Guid to the mound, who was more than up for the task. He struck out ten and shut down the Brewers over the first seven, for his twenty-second win of the year. Fish came in and saved it, for his fourteenth of the year. Hendy gave us all the runs we needed early by leading off the game with his twenty-fourth homer of the season.

Toronto lost again, and it was an ex-Met, Walt Terrell, who shut 'em out 2–0. The magic number is still two. Three more wins and the pennant would be ours.

Friday, October 4 — TORONTO

As usual, we were out of starters to go with tonight, so Billy was forced to use Whit, who was making his first appearance since their slugging match a week and half ago.

Whit, who had cleared his differences with Billy, gave it his best, but it wasn't good enough. The Jays scored two unearned runs off him in the fifth and Billy took him out and brought in Scurry, who had been pitching for us like Cy Young since we'd gotten him from Pittsburgh.

Unfortunately, he gave up a run in the eighth to make it 3–2 Toronto, and we at once found ourselves breathing our last breaths. They had their big guy on the mound, this kid named Henke, who'd just been phenomenal the second half of the season. Things looked dim, but we were used to that around here and we responded in the fashion that Billy had taught us, we fought back.

With two outs in the ninth, we sent our last hope up to the plate to face Henke, who had mowed down all five batters that he had faced in the game. The aled-up crowd was goin' crazy, cheering at every pitch—and in nineteen different languages, to boot.

But Wynegar was deaf to the noise and the tension. All that graced his face was a stunning look of determination. Then Butch lofted a 1–1 pitch to right field that at first looked to be playable, but it quickly disappeared over the fence for only his fifth homer of the year—his first since a few weeks before he got beaned in the on-deck circle back in June. The stadium full of once-cheering fans grew silent.

Meach was the next batter. He hit a quick grounder to Damaso Garcia at second, which the second baseman stopped but threw wildly. Meach was safe. Hendy then drew a walk off a shaken Henke, which brought Donny, the league's leading RBI man to the plate.

He lofted a lazy fly ball to centerfield. It looked like the third and last out. It looked like the end of our dreams for a pennant. But Lloyd Moseby, the Jays' center-fielder, lost the ball in the lights or the moon or somethin' and looked like one of those Canadian fans in the stands trying to catch a foul ball.

The ball trickled off his glove and fell to the ground. Meach, running all the way, scored easily. There was still hope for our dreams, for my dream, and for the dream that I had for my dad, who was progressing but who was still very ill and still in intensive care. My thoughts were still on him every minute.

Saturday, October 5 — TORONTO

Ernie Whitt took Cowls deep in the second inning to give the Jays a 1–0 lead. Then in the third, Moseby and Cecil Upshaw followed suit with a pair of back-to-back homers, and we instantly found ourselves down 3–0.

We scratched and we fought but the most we could get off of Doyle Alexander, who George is still paying off a contract on, was one run, which Winnie drove in. Once Alexander got a lead, he was just sensational and it was over just as quick as that. We lost 5–1 and my dream died with it, or so I thought.

Monday, October 7—WHEELING, W. VA.

After an all night partying session with our buddies here in New York, Joe and I packed and left for Pittsburgh.

When we walked into my dad's room that day, his face just lit right up. He saw the cap and ball from my three hundredth that I had promised to bring him. Tears filled all our eyes as I placed the cap on his head and put the ball in his hand. We talked for awhile until he got tired, and just before we left, he fell asleep. But shortly before doin' so, he slid the ball, his fingers still wrapped tightly around it, underneath the covers of his bed for safekeeping.

Tuesday, October 8—ATLANTA

After I got home, I surely expected to hear from Ted. From all the news I'd been hearing for so long, I thought that I stood a pretty good chance of being named the club's manager.

Ted's pledge that I would someday manage his ball club just kept rolling around inside my head. Even the Yankees thought that Ted would offer me the job. That's basically why they hadn't offered me anything for next season. They just wanted to see if Ted was gonna do anything first.

Wednesday, October 9—ATLANTA

Chuck Tanner was named as the Braves' new manager today. I'm at best dejected, disappointed, and hurt. I realize that Chuck is one of the top managers in the game, but I thought I'd hear something from Ted, at least telling me that he was gonna hire Chuck.

Thursday, October 10—ATLANTA

Chuck was asked the one question that was on everyone's mind concerning the ball club: Will Niekro be back? According to Chuck, I will be. He said today that he'd like to have me on his pitching staff. But, then, he always did want me. In fact, he was the one pushing Pittsburgh to sign me two years ago.

Friday, October 11—ATLANTA

My old buddy Bobby Cox was named general manager of the Braves today. With Bobby, Chuck, and Ted makin' the decisions, I'd have to think that I stand a pretty good chance of being signed by the Braves.

Tuesday, October 15 — WHEELING

I flew back up here early yesterday. My dad is in trouble again. He just had three successive heart attacks. Again, it doesn't look good.

Nancy called me this afternoon to say that Bobby Cox announced today that the Braves had no interest at all in me. Which I find kinda strange. With a pitching staff like theirs, it seems odd not to be interested in a sixteen-game winner.

I was somewhat disappointed by their decision, but I didn't let myself get too down, 'cause right now, I have more important things to worry about. But this is just how things go at my age. As an athlete, you're discriminated against. But why? Certainly not because of my numbers.

Hell, I've won a total of thirty-two games the last two years. Only a few guys in all the big leagues have won as many or more. But, yet, I'm unwanted. And I'll tell ya, it sure isn't because of my credentials. How could it be?

No, it's because of my age. In fact, I bet if you listed all the pitchers in the bigs by their stats only and gave each manager an opportunity to choose ten pitchers, I'd appear on each manager's list. That is, of course, until they took a peek at my age. Then I'd be gone as fast as they could scratch my name off their lists.

They're all scared that I'm gonna die on the mound or somethin'. Bullshit! Let the stats speak for themselves. Let my value be gauged upon productivity, not age. But that's not how the system works! That's not how it's run! And because of that, I'm out of a job.

Unfortunately, I've got to admit there may not be room for me on anyone's roster next year, and that my three hundredth win may have been the last time that I'd ever take the mound. It just isn't fair. All that I can hope for is that someone will see the light, see through all the bullshit, and give me another chance.

January 8, 1986 — ATLANTA

I signed my contract with the Yanks, the only club to even show any interest in me. I gave them the same deal I would have given the Braves; I'll play for whatever they care to pay me.

It looks like I've got something to prove once again. TOO OLD MY ASS!